welcome
to a year like no other

The Arts

Nosta

MOVES WITH THE TIMES

POOL OF

OLD
ever chang

centre of the
creative universe

FILM

A winning spirit
Passion

determination
skill

DYNAMIC

Everton

sharp

radical
crucial

PENDENT

resh
re

Carlsberg

Warren Bradley
Leader of Liverpool City Council and
Deputy Chairman of Liverpool Culture Company

Bryan Gray
Chairman of Liverpool
Culture Company

Phil Redmond
Creative Director and Deputy Chairman
of Liverpool Culture Company

"Welcome to Liverpool, European Capital of Culture 2008. The programme in your hands charts the work of literally thousands of people who have been enthused, energised and inspired to showcase their creativity in countless ways during '08. It is a year which offers internationally-acclaimed work and community projects. It reflects the city's edgy spirit and sense of fun. Liverpool is unique because of its people. They - and you - are the focus of this year of celebration. Come with us and enjoy Liverpool '08."

Opening for '08

On the weekend of 11-12 January Liverpool celebrates the beginning of its reign as European Capital Culture 2008, with two unique, headline events:

11 January
The People's Launch
St George's Plateau, Lime Street

At 20:08 on the 11th, the artists and people of the city gather together on St George's Plateau. Here, the official **People's Launch** will include an extraordinary performance from the rooftops surrounding this cultural heart of the city. This spectacular event involves massed community choirs and aerialists, performers ranging from Ringo Starr to The Wombats and an epic aerial ballet of dancing cranes, containers and scissor lifts, as Liverpool celebrates the transformation of the 'Big Dig' into the 'Big Gig'.

World Capital of Pop

THAT SOMETHING CHORUS
THAT MELODY

12 January
Liverpool - The Musical
ECHO Arena Liverpool, Kings Dock

Created specially to open Liverpool's new 10,600-seat arena, **Liverpool - The Musical** celebrates both the past and the future of the city. Integrating live performance and film in a radical new way and vertically stacking performers seven stories into the air, the show features a once-in-a-lifetime cast including: Vasily Petrenko and the Royal Liverpool Philharmonic Orchestra in collaboration with: No Fakin DJs, Ringo Starr, Echo and The Bunnymen, Ian Broudie, The Farm, Riuven, The Wombats, Pete Wylie, Dave Stewart and the people of the city.

"I'm very excited about Liverpool being European Capital of Culture in '08. We have a fantastic series of events which are sure to get you excited too. I'm very proud of the city and I look forward to welcoming you all and showing you a good time. It's going to be great year in a very special place."

Sir Paul McCartney

A year in Music

Think of Liverpool and one art form, above all others, springs to mind... music.

Liverpool displayed a powerful musical personality long before the sixties, the Beat Generation and four lads who shook the world.

The port of Liverpool is mentioned in more seafaring music than any other city. It is home to one of the UK's oldest orchestras and has welcomed music from around the globe, producing an annual festival programme celebrating Irish, Arabic and African influences as well as home-grown festivals like the Summer Pops, Mathew Street and Creamfields.

While the Royal Liverpool Philharmonic has commissioned a record 30 new compositions for '08, Liverpool also hosts the nation's newest and most exciting festival of contemporary pop - Liverpool Music Week (LMW).

In '08 LMW links with Liverpool Electric, which will plug into the BBC Electric Proms and MTV Europe Music Awards, to create two weeks of the most vibrant indie, electro, hip-hop and rock you'll hear on the planet.

This feast of music by artists from 'across the universe' together with local musicians in special projects, new commissions and large-scale concerts makes for a year in music to echo down the ages.

8 highlights in 08

1 - 5 January, 7.00pm
Emilia di Liverpool
St George's Concert Room, William Brown Street

Elena Tzavara, director
Elisabetta Pian, set designer

Donizetti's romantic invention of 1824, set among the mountains and alpine valleys of the city, receives a fresh makeover by The European Opera Centre.

Two casts of talented young European singers and an orchestra, drawn from around Europe, including Liverpool's associate Cities on the Edge, (see page 164) are brought together under the musical direction of Giovanni Pacor of the Fondazione Arena di Verona.

St George's Concert Room hosts six performances of the city's very own opera. There will be a special people's performance for the city at 3pm on New Year's Day.

liverpool08.com

5 January, 7.30pm
The Wayne Shorter Quartet
with the Royal Liverpool Philharmonic Orchestra (RLPO)

Philharmonic Hall, Hope Street

Clark Rundell, conductor
Danilo Perez, piano
John Patitucci, bass
Brian Blade, drums

Fusion pioneer and seven-time Grammy award-winner Wayne Shorter, a tenor and soprano saxophonist without equal, steps into the acoustic realm in a special collaboration with the RLPO.

Having successfully replaced John Coltrane as saxophonist in The Miles Davis Quintet, Shorter's legend was cemented when he left to form the seminal Weather Report, collaborating with those at the forefront of jazz and pop.

Here Shorter and his Quartet performs orchestral arrangements of self-penned classics, including Speak No Evil, Penelope, Infant Eyes, Witch Hunt, Adam's Apple and Footprints.

This performance is part of the Fresh Festival (3 - 5 January), featuring live gigs with a compelling line-up of local, national and international artists, forging new ground and creating new work together.

fresh-festival.co.uk

28 February, 7.30pm

Tavener Requiem

Liverpool Metropolitan Cathedral
of Christ the King, Mount Pleasant

WORLD PREMIERE

Commissioned by Liverpool Culture Company for '08

Royal Liverpool Philharmonic Orchestra
Vasily Petrenko and Ian Tracey, conductors
Royal Liverpool Philharmonic Choir
Josephine Knight, cello Andrew Kennedy, tenor

Sir John Tavener's new Requiem is an attempt to reconcile the world's warring religions through music and contemplation of the final journey that we all share.

Within the circular nave of the cathedral, four groups of performers, set out in the shape of a cross, will represent the four great faiths of Christianity, Hinduism, Judaism and Islam. A solo cello in their midst will symbolise the 'Primordial Light' from which we take our starting-point and to which we all return at the end.

"I envisage the final movement as a huge affirmation of the ONENESS of God, as all four groups pulsate round a vast building singing 'I AM' in Hebrew, Sanskrit, Arabic and Greek."

Sir John Tavener

liverpoolphil.com

1 March, 7.30pm

St David's Day Concert
Liverpool Welsh Choral Union with Aled Jones

Philharmonic Hall, Hope Street

Keith Orrell, conductor

The Liverpool Welsh Choral Union celebrate St David's Day in style with one of its most famous Welshmen, presenter and singer Aled Jones, coupled with the stylish playing of the RLPO.

liverpoolphil.com

14 - 15 March

The Long Walk

The Great Hall, Haigh Street

Commissioned by Liverpool Culture Company for '08

The Long Walk is a new composition from the acclaimed community music organisation More Music.

It is a response to the tragedy of February '04 when more than 23 Chinese cockle-pickers died after becoming trapped by rising tides on Morecambe Bay.

First performed in March '07 it has been rewritten and recreated with people in Liverpool.

It showcases an orchestra of professional musicians and community participants in a musical offering that explores displacement, exploitation and journey.

thelongwalk.info

Also in February: TWINS p 050 and Chinese New Year Celebrations p 068

15 March, 7.30pm

Karl Jenkins
Stabat Mater

Liverpool Cathedral, St James Mount

WORLD PREMIERE

Bach, Komm, Jesu, Komm, BWV 299
Bach, Jesu meine Freude, BWV 227
Karl Jenkins, Stabat Mater (World Premiere)
Karl Jenkins, conductor
Royal Liverpool Philharmonic Orchestra
Royal Liverpool Philharmonic Choir
Ian Tracey, director

Commissioned by the Royal Liverpool
Philharmonic for '08

Welsh musician Karl Jenkins (below) is a true original who initially made his mark in jazz and rock. Following his No1 classical album - Requiem, his next major work deals with the suffering of Mary, Jesus Christ's mother, during his crucifixion.

This '13th Century' Latin poem has been set to music by many composers, but Jenkins' is a new approach.

liverpoolphil.com

"Everything I write stems back from my classical background. That's where... my inspiration is from. My heroes are Wagner, Strauss and Mahler: they produced the best music ever written."

Karl Jenkins

30 March

European Union
Youth Orchestra

Conducted by Vladimir Ashkenazy

Philharmonic Hall, Hope Street

Presented by Liverpool Culture Company for '08

Peer Gynt, Suite No. 1
Sibelius, Violin Concerto
Strauss, Symphonia Domestica
Vladimir Ashkenazy, conductor
Arabella Steinbacher, violin

One of the world's most prestigious orchestras - the EUYO - is here conducted by its Music Director, Maestro Vladimir Ashkenazy for the final leg of its '08 European Tour.

liverpoolphil.com

7 March - December

Twilight City
The Hive Collective

Various venues

A Liverpool Commission

Commissioned by Liverpool Culture Company for '08

The Hive Collective has been at the forefront of electronic music and audiovisual performance since '03, working with the scene's most innovative performers.

Hive Twilight City is a series of four, high-profile audiovisual performances in tribute to Liverpool's industrial and business buildings, bricks and plate glass; the iconic and the mundane, the city centre and the suburbs.

Culminating with a CD and publication, each audiovisual performance provides a snapshot prior to the city's mutation: familiar sounds reworked, familiar sights distorted.

The first Hive Collective event will be at the Leaf Warehouse on Friday 7 March at 8pm. Featuring Jah Wobble - Jaki Liebezeit - Philip Jeck, Shackleton, The Bug feat. Warrior Queen, King Klang.

DJ's Furness, Venom, Dreadnought, DJ Alextronic, Hive visual artists.

thehivecollective.co.uk
ticketweb.co.uk

17 - 18 April

Into the Little Hill

A lyric tale in two parts

Pacific Road Arts Centre, Birkenhead

UK PREMIERE

Commissioned by Liverpool Culture Company for '08

George Benjamin, music
Martin Crimp, text
Daniel Jeanneteau, director
Marie-Christine Soma, light design
and artistic collaboration
Franck Ollu, conductor

The Pied Piper story gets a political updating as a minister tries to reassure a restless voting public by commissioning an extermination of rats.

It's a tale with many dark and sinister implications, as the rats are spirited away by the ghostly stranger.

Nobody claims responsibility for their vanishing, but when the latter refuses to pay up; the stranger abducts the children and takes them 'into the little hill'.

"Entrancingly beautiful... more ravishing than anyone could possibly have imagined."

The Guardian

Commissioned by: The Festival d'Automne à Paris in association with the Ernst von Siemens Music Foundation, the Opéra National de Paris, the Ensemble Modern together with the Forberg Schneider Foundation.

Coproduction: Festival d'Automne à Paris, Opéra national de Paris, T&M, Oper Frankfurt, Lincoln Center Festival, Wienerfestwochen, Holland Festival, Ensemble Modern, Liverpool Culture Company.

liverpool08.com

1 May

Ecce Cor Meum

Liverpool Cathedral, St James Mount

NORTHERN CHARITY PREMIERE

Kate Royal, soloist
Gavin Greenaway, conductor
Royal Liverpool Philharmonic Orchestra and Choir
Liverpool Cathedral Choir

Sir Paul McCartney brings Ecce Cor Meum, (Behold my Heart), one of his conceptually and logistically audacious projects, to Liverpool.

More than eight years in the making it's a work written in the style of sacred English Choral Music, a tradition dating back 500 years.

A piece of spiritual music, written in part after the passing of his wife Linda, Ecce Cor Meum is the first piece of music McCartney has written to include a children's chorus.

The title was inspired by the inscription McCartney noticed above a statue of Christ in St Ignatius Church, New York City. The reference in the church context is to the Sacred Heart of Jesus, although McCartney freely adapted the text for use in his composition.

WINNER: Best Album - 2007 Classical Brits

liverpoolphil.com
liverpoolcathedral.org.uk
paulmccartney.com

Also in April: One Step Forward, One Step Back p 092 and Viennese Balls p 093

fresh
real
what rules
SEMINAL
literature
AN EVER-CHANGING CANVAS

17 May, 7.30pm

An Evening with Bryn Terfel

Philharmonic Hall, Hope Street

Royal Liverpool Philharmonic Orchestra
Vasily Petrenko, conductor
Bryn Terfel, bass-baritone
Royal Liverpool Philharmonic Choir

Bryn Terfel is one of the world's hottest properties in opera, while his albums of show songs by Rodgers & Hammerstein and Lerner & Loewe have become bestsellers.

"Whatever the mysterious qualities are that make for a great voice, Bryn Terfel has them in spades." The Times

liverpoolphil.com

24 May, 7.30 pm

Voices Across the Ocean
Liverpool Welsh Choral

Mossley Hill Parish Church, Rose Lane

Conductor, Keith Orrell

Liverpool Welsh Choral and members of the world-famous Pro Arte Chorale, New York, share beautiful music from both sides of the Big Pond.

The programme will include Rutter's sublime Requiem and Bernstein's spectacular Chichester Psalms. The choirs will be joined by treble James Orrell, organist Stephen Hargreaves and a small instrumental ensemble.

lwcu.co.uk

29 May - 1 June

Southport International Jazz Festival
Various venues

ANNUAL EVENT

With over 80% of the concerts free, this festival is a huge hit every year.

Most jazz styles are featured over the four days including trad, gypsy, latin, big band and funk as well as contemporary and more avant-garde artistes.

Venues include the Town Hall gardens and Wayfarers Arcade as well as theatres, restaurants and café bars and concerts taking place all day and all night.

sefton.gov.uk/arts

1 June

The Liverpool Sound

Anfield Stadium, Anfield Road

This spectacular multi-artist concert headlined by Sir Paul McCartney, is a once-in-a-lifetime event to celebrate Liverpool's status as the World Capital of Pop.

And where better to celebrate that special connection between Liverpool's twin loves - football and music - than on the pitch at Anfield in front of 30,000 people?

Raised on rock 'n' roll, rhythm and blues, and soul from across the Atlantic, Liverpool created an exciting new sound all of its own in the early sixties.

Merseybeat rang around the world and was introduced to large parts of this nation via the choir on the Kop. But the biggest sound of all, that has never stopped influencing the world of music, is that of The Beatles.

This concert is about defining that unique Liverpool Sound and how it changed the face of popular music forever.

As a live broadcast, this concert will feature a great Anfield atmosphere as well as performances from locations showcasing Liverpool's World Heritage architecture.

Liverpool's music culture has travelled around the world. In '08, it's getting back - to be redefined where it began.

liverpool08.com

4 - 14 June
Festival of Hope '08
Hope Street

Food stalls, dancers, music, artists, choirs and bands from USA, Africa, India, Europe and Liverpool take over the street that links the city's two cathedrals.

The final day boasts an extravagant street pageant by church communities from across the region, and involves music ranging from traditional gospel to hip-hop, rap and soul.

There will also be a spectacular gospel concert on 13 June, spearheaded by City Sings Gospel, from Liverpool Lighthouse in the heart of Anfield.

Liverpool Lighthouse also hosts a National Gospel Music Exhibition from 3 - 30 June.

liverpoollighthouse.com

28 June, 7.30pm
War Requiem
by Benjamin Britten

Liverpool Cathedral, St James Mount

Commissioned by Liverpool Culture Company for '08

Royal Liverpool Philharmonic Orchestra
Ian Tracey and Eberhard Metternich, conductors
Lada Biriucov, soprano
Ian Bostridge, tenor
Hanno Mueller-Brachman, bass
Royal Liverpool Philharmonic Choir, Choir of Liverpool Cathedral, Choir of Liverpool Metropolitan Cathedral, Choir of Cologne Cathedral

One of the 20th century's greatest choral works was commissioned to celebrate the consecration in 1962 of the rebuilt Coventry Cathedral, destroyed during the Second World War.

Dedicated to the memory of four of Britten's school friends, three of whom died in the 1939-1945 conflict, the War Requiem combines the war poems of Wilfred Owen with the Latin Mass for the Dead.

Collaborating with Cologne, Liverpool's twin city, where a performance will also be given by these same forces, the Royal Liverpool Philharmonic is reflecting and celebrating Britten's passionate desire for healing and reconciliation between former enemies.

liverpoolphil.com
liverpoolcathedral.org.uk

21 - 22 June
Africa Oyé
Sefton Park, Liverpool

ANNUAL EVENT

Africa Oyé is the UK's largest, free celebration of African music and culture and takes place annually in Liverpool.

Now in its sixteenth year, Africa Oyé is about more than music. Stalls selling the best food, drink, Arts and Crafts and fashion from Africa and beyond will again be present at the Oyé village and there will also be face painting, bouncy castles, and a mobile climbing wall to keep the kids happy.

Oyé 2008 will be recorded by BBC Radio 3 and The Africa Channel (Sky channel 281) for future broadcast in the UK, Africa and The Caribbean.

africaoye.com
myspace.com/africaoye

5 July

Chinese Dub

30 Hertz Records and Jah Wobble

Carling Academy, Hotham Street

WORLD PREMIERE

A Liverpool Commission

Commissioned by Liverpool Culture Company for '08

Internationally-acclaimed musician Jah Wobble has worked with music icons such as Björk, Brian Eno, Massive Attack, Baaba Mal and Natasha Atlas.

He now joins forces with the Pagoda Chinese Youth Orchestra (PCYO) for an innovative musical collaboration to promote Chinese music to a wider audience.

July '08 also marks the 25th birthday for the PCYO, Europe's first and largest Chinese youth orchestra.

30hertzrecords.com
liverpool-academy.co.uk

18 - 21 July

International Shanty Festival

Liverpool Albert and Wellington Docks

This world leading showcase of maritime songs and music, takes place in conjunction with the start of The Tall Ships' Races (see page 143). Styles range from cajun, celtic, folk-rock and authentic traditional, performed on ships, stages and indoor venues across the city centre.

liverpool08.com

Throughout July

Liverpool Summer Pops

ECHO Arena Liverpool, Kings Dock

ANNUAL EVENT

Held every July and attracting over 100,000 music fans, Summer Pops has developed into one of England's premier music festivals. The roster of acts since 2001 reads like a who's who of contemporary music, including Bob Dylan, Paul Simon, Elton John, Diana Ross and The Who.

cmpentertainment.com

23 August

Creamfields '08

Daresbury, Cheshire

ANNUAL EVENT

One of the UK's favourite electronic, live music festivals celebrates its 10th anniversary in a tranquil setting on the outskirts of Merseyside. This global award-winning event will boast a 'world-class' running order in '08 across the electronica spectrum, ranging from house, electro, drum and bass, breaks, nu rave, techno, trance, hardhouse and beyond. Listen out for live broadcasts on BBC Radio One.

creamfieldsfestival.co.uk

24 - 25 August

Mathew Street Music Festival

Liverpool city centre

ANNUAL EVENT

Europe's largest, free, annual, city centre music festival celebrates Liverpool's music heritage, but also showcasing talent from all over the world.

liverpool08.com

Also in July: The Beat Goes On p 156: Also in August: Brouhaha Carnival Procession p 074

4 September, 7.30pm

Berliner Philharmoniker

Philharmonic Hall, Hope Street

Presented by Liverpool Culture Company for '08

Sir Simon Rattle, conductor

Wagner Prelude and Liebestod Tristan and Isolde
Messiaen Turangalila Symphony

Sir Simon Rattle brings the 'internationally-acclaimed' Berliner Philharmoniker to his Liverpool home.

Nothing else in the classical repertoire can compare to Messiaen's Turangalila live, even more significantly in '08, his centenary year, when celebration concerts will take place across the world.

A massive orchestra including piano and ondes Martenot combine in this larger-than-life tribute to love along with Wagner's Prelude and Liebestod.

This concert by the Berliner Philharmoniker has been made possible by the support of the Deutsche Bank.

"The greatest orchestra in the world." The Guardian

liverpoolphil.com

15 - 20 September

Audiovision

**Mersey Tunnel Air Vent (AV),
George's Dock Building, Pier Head**

A Liverpool Commission

Commissioned by Liverpool Culture Company for '08

Liverpool's first international audiovisual (AV) festival sees local and international artists utilising the visual capacities of the Art Deco landmark - the Mersey Tunnel Air Vent.

Kinetophone Records will host video installations, AV performances, film screenings and AV workshops as artists transform the air-vent into a spectacular array of colour, light and sound.

Responding to Liverpool's cityscape, a public programme of workshops will also be staged, including a range of training events, master classes and the showcasing of work for a public audience. These events will be delivered by Neutral Spoon.

kineticfallacy.co.uk

Throughout '08

Milapfest

Various events city wide

ANNUAL EVENT

Highlights for '08 include:

Onam Festival - 12 September

Celebrate Indian culture with this popular harvest festival from Kerala in South India.

Navratri - 29 September - 8 October

The nine-day festival of Navratri is a unique and colourful community event where people of all ages, religions, and backgrounds are invited to participate in the Gujarati folk dances of Garba and Raas.

Music for the Mind and Soul

On the last Saturday of each month at the Philharmonic Hall. Free of charge and allows audiences to enjoy a variety of Indian music styles while trying out delicious Indian food.

milapfest.com

Also in September: Tour of Britain Finale p 147 and Heritage Open Days p 159

2 October

Royal Liverpool Philharmonic Orchestra

Philharmonic Hall, Hope Street

WORLD PREMIERE

Sir Simon Rattle, conductor

Brett Dean - World Premiere
Sibelius Symphony No 5

Commissioned by Liverpool Culture Company for '08

One of Liverpool's favourite sons comes home to conduct this great orchestra in the concert hall where he began his stellar music career.

The programme includes a new work by Brett Dean, one of the most internationally performed composers of his generation.

Simon Rattle is a leading interpreter of Dean's music. Dean currently holds the position of Artistic Director of the Australian National Academy of Music.

liverpoolphil.com

25 October

Karl Jenkins
Liverpool Welsh Choral Union

Philharmonic Hall, Hope Street

Commissioned by Liverpool Welsh Choral Union for '08

WORLD PREMIERE

World-famous (and Liverpool Welsh Choral Union Patron) Karl Jenkins conducts the first performance of a new work with the Royal Liverpool Philharmonic Orchestra.

liverpoolphil.com

17 October - 2 November

Liverpool Irish Festival

Various venues

ANNUAL EVENT

The festival celebrates the unique link between Liverpool and Ireland. Started in '03, it now attracts over 15,000 people across more than 60 events, over six weeks. Headliners have previously included concerts by Van Morrison, a play by Donal O'Kelly and talks by Jimmy McGovern.

Highlights for '08:

17 October, 7.30pm

Burial at Thebes

Philharmonic Hall, Hope Street

Seamus Heaney, poet
Dominique le Gendre, composer
Derek Walcott, director
Peter Manning, conductor
Manning Camerata

This 1,000 year-old Greek tragedy has been updated as a modern day allegory of politics and power.

It is also the first time Nobel Prize winner, Seamus Heaney (right), has exposed his own great work to musical interpretation.

Composer Dominique Le Gendre will use the orchestra, soloists and chorus to recreate the action in Heaney's epic poem with dramatic narration by Trinidadian Rapso, played by the actor Wendell Manwarren.

"It will be a truly stunning event... the vision to bring one of the world's greatest stories to a musical setting offers a rare opportunity for a work of considerable importance and beauty to be seen and heard." Derek Walcott

liverpoolphil.com
liverpoolirishfestival.com

19 October

Christy Moore

Philharmonic Hall, Hope Street

Irish legend, folk singer Christy Moore is welcomed back to perform in one of his favourite cities, with his style of mixing traditional songs with contemporary observations of social and political aspects of Irish life. Adding elements of rock and popular music to well-crafted, tradition-based tunes, he has been a major inspiration to Irish modern artists such as U2, the Pogues and Sinead O'Connor.

"Every year in Liverpool is a year of culture."

Christy Moore

liverpoolphil.com
liverpoolirishfestival.com

Also in October: King Lear p 101 and Le Corbusier, Art of Architecture p 160

22 - 26 October

Liverpool Electric
as part of BBC Electric Proms

Various venues
liverpool08.com

1 - 16 November

Liverpool Music Week
Various venues
ANNUAL EVENT

liverpoolmusicweek.co.uk

6 November

MTV Europe Music Awards

ECHO Arena Liverpool, Kings Dock

mtv.com

For two weeks Liverpool will once again be at the centre of the musical universe when it showcases an incredible programme of musical talent - culminating in the MTV Europe Music Awards.

The fortnight begins with the launch of Liverpool Electric, which plugs into the BBC Electric Proms. It will be the festival's third year and the first time it has had a presence outside London - rightly paying homage to the UK's foremost musical city.

And if that's not enough '08 sees the biggest Liverpool Music Week to date. Established with a single event in '03, it is now the UK's largest indoor festival.

Liverpool Electric, Liverpool Music Week and the MTV Europe Music Awards - dates that will be etched on every music fan's radar in autumn '08.

ANTHEMIC
The pulse
the beat
jazz

7 - 25 November

The International Guitar Festival of Great Britain

Presented by Wirral Borough Council

Pacific Road Arts Centre, Birkenhead
and various venues

ANNUAL EVENT

Now in its 20th year, this three-week autumn festival attracts a plethcra of performers from all over the world.

The UK's longest-established annual guitar festival has something for everyone's tastes, with an eclectic - and sometimes electric - mix of blues, folk, rock, jazz, flamenco and classical from a diverse range of world-class guitarists.

Highlights include lunchtime recitals in Hamilton Square and concerts in Birkenhead's medieval Priory - the oldest building on Merseyside - complete with mulled wine.

Other concerts take place in pubs, ferry buildings, theatres, warehouses, concert halls, art galleries and even a double-decker bus.

bestguitarfest.com
pacificroad.co.uk

19 November – 6 December
Cornerstone Festival
The Cornerstone, Haigh Street

ANNUAL EVENT

This festival is now in its seventh year and is based in Everton, home to Liverpool Hope University's Creative & Performing Arts Centre. A special focus of the festival is the presentation of newly created work in the fields of music, dance, theatre, writing, comedy and visual arts.

"The best of more than a dozen city-based festivals." Liverpool Echo

Highlights for '08 include:

18 - 20 November
Le Nouvel Ensemble Moderne
The Cornerstone, Haigh Street

New work for Le NEM

Commissioned by Liverpool Culture Company for '08

Founded in 1989 by pianist and conductor Lorraine Vaillancourt, Le NEM is a chamber orchestra of 15 musicians nurtured on the classics of the 20th century.

Ensemble-in-residence at the faculty of music of the Université de Montréal, their performance at the Cornerstone Festival includes a work by the winner of a new composers competition.

This competition is organised by Liverpool Culture Company, Cornerstone Festival, Ensemble 10.10, with assistance from the society for the promotion of new music.

cornerstonefestival.com

21 November
The Only Moving Thing
Presented by eighth blackbird
The Cornerstone, Haigh Street

UK PREMIERE

Commissioned by Liverpool Culture Company for '08

The Only Moving Thing features new commissions by Steve Reich and Bang on a Can founders David Lang, Michael Gordon and Julia Wolfe.

In Reich's double sextet, eighth blackbird performs simultaneously live and pre-recorded; while Lang/Wolfe/Gordon's 'singing in the dead of night' is a 45-minute suite conceived in collaboration with seminal New York choreographer Susan Marshall who will direct the movement.

Debuting in spring '08 in the USA, this programme will tour internationally in the '08/'09 season.

"Steve Reich is among just a handful of living composers who can legitimately claim to have altered the direction of musical history."

The Guardian

cornerstonefestival.com

December
The Rightful Owners of the Song

Philharmonic Hall, Hope Street

A Liverpool Commission

Commissioned by Liverpool Culture Company for '08

Inspired by Brian Patten's poem, 'The Rightful Owners of The Song' is a simple idea...

Discover and bring together a group of Liverpool's best pub-singers, karaoke-hosts and professional or semi-professional singers for a one-off performance, with the Royal Liverpool Philharmonic Orchestra.

liverpool08.com

6 - 7 December
BBC Radio 3 Choir of the Year

Philharmonic Hall, Hope Street

Category Finals

Choir of the Year, the UK's largest amateur singing competition, was launched in 1984 to provide a nationwide shop window for the best of amateur singing groups.

Since the competition began 120,000 singers from over 2,000 choirs have taken part.

Open to all, the competition is free.

choiroftheyear.co.uk

Also in December: The Penny Readings p 041 and Portrait of a Nation p 163

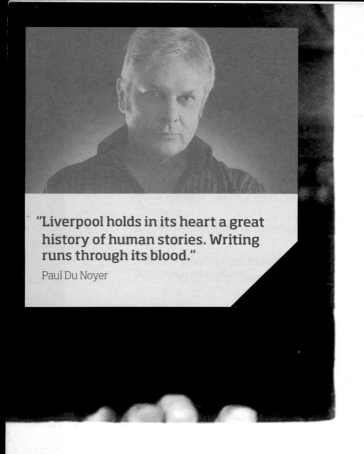

"Liverpool holds in its heart a great history of human stories. Writing runs through its blood."

Paul Du Noyer

A year in Literature

Liverpool has long been a fertile ground for literature - from salty tales to the traditional folklore of its multi-cultural population.

It is a city famed for writing that champions the underdog and highlights injustice, that exposes the underbelly of society, that makes us laugh and makes us cry.

This spirit is in the plays and scripts of Bleasdale, McGovern, Lane, La Plante, Redmond and Russell.

It is in the poetry of Henri, McGough and Patten, Tafari and Feinstein.

It is in the novels of Bainbridge, Barker, Forrester and Cottrell Boyce.

To celebrate this tradition, Liverpool aims to showcase and develop the emerging voices of the next generation.

the Bluecoat continues to support the written word when it re-opens in '08 with a writing festival scheduled for October amongst its highlights.

New writing has also been restored to centre stage in Liverpool's theatres, forming the core of the Everyman programme, with the popular Everyword new writing festival.

In '08, Liverpool will ensure this literary output continues to be as thrilling as ever.

8 highlights in

To 31 January
Astrid Lingren
Exhibition

Picton Library Reading Room, William Brown Street

This exhibition commemorates the 100th anniversary of the birth of the writer responsible for the Pippi Longstocking books.

There will be Pippi Longstocking workshops/story sessions for January.

Liverpool libraries in conjunction with the Swedish Embassy.

liverpool.gov.uk/libraries

6 March onwards
Liverpool Reads
City wide

ANNUAL EVENT

This city-wide reading initiative aims to create a community of readers through the shared medium of a book.

Since '05 a book is selected and distributed for free across the city.

For '08, the city will be reading the novels 'Keeper' and 'Tamar', by award-winning author Mal Peet.

A programme of school and community projects, reading groups, and public events accompanies the 'big read'.

Expect exciting author events and other activities from 6 March (World Book Day) onwards.

liverpoolreads.com

Also in January: The People's Launch p 010: Also in February: Anima p 090

7 - 12 April

Wirral Bookfest

Venues around Wirral

ANNUAL EVENT

A celebration of books of all kinds, this week-long festival will be based around Wirral's libraries.

The festival includes poetry, local history and genealogy, big authors such as Brian Jacques (right), performers, murder mystery, an event around films based on books and even a look at graphic novels.

There will be plenty of opportunities to get involved, with workshops, competitions and a special family day for all ages.

wirral.gov.uk/libraries

Late April - early May

Poetry in the City

Various venues

ANNUAL EVENT

Poetry in the City (PiC) is a collaboration between several poetry organisations, promoters and performance nights working collectively to raise the profile of poetry in Liverpool.

Through commissions for new work, translations, and interaction across other art forms and new media, PiC offers many opportunities to get involved in the city's lively poetry scene.

The festival will feature a diverse programme of performances and events: slam poetry, open mics, workshops, games and installations.

Indoors and outdoors, the '08 festival will include nationally-acclaimed award-winners and innovative experimentalists such as Liverpool's Levi Tafari (left), Mohammad Khalil and Eleanor Rees.

PiC is organised by Dead Good Poets Society, Modern Transmissions (University of Liverpool), Back in the Machine Gun, Orbis International Library Journal, The Windows Project and Liverpool John Moores University.

poetryinthecity.co.uk
headlandpublications.co.uk

Also in March: Stabat Mater p 018: Also in April: AL and AL p 051 and Ken Dodd and Liverpool's Laughter Makers p 122

May

Writing on the Wall Festival

Various venues

ANNUAL EVENT

Writing on the Wall (WoW) is an annual programme of events culminating in a festival.

Schools, young people, local communities and broader audiences, celebrate writing, diversity, tolerance, story-telling and humour through controversy, inquiry and debate.

WoW brings established writers and performers into the city to work alongside local artists and members of Liverpool's diverse communities, producing new and innovative work.

writingonthewall.org.uk

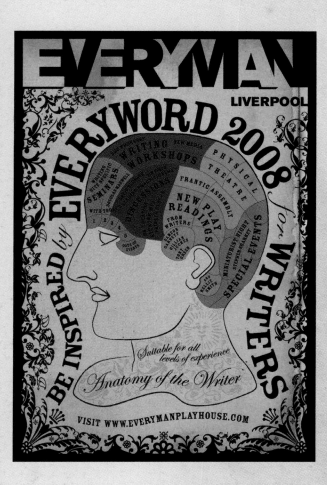

15 - 26 July

Everyword

Everyman Theatre, Hope Street

ANNUAL EVENT

The Everyman's annual, new writing festival returns bigger and better than ever before.

Extended to two weeks in '08, Everyword offers a feast of seminars, workshops, discussions and rehearsed readings.

The festival also enables aspiring writers to work with and learn from some of the country's leading practitioners.

Catch a first glimpse of new work in development and pieces by some of the city's leading writers.

everymanplayhouse.com

August

Community Shakespeare
Presented by The Reader

Birkenhead Park, Wirral

Inspired by a grass-roots Shakespeare season in New York's Central Park (which was modelled on Birkenhead Park, below) 'the bard' comes to the Wirral to celebrate '08.

Under the eye of a professional director, volunteers perform a three-night open-air production of 'The Winter's Tale'.

There's always an open invitation to play, or make music, or costumes, or design the tickets, or staple programmes, put the chairs out, or sell the ice-creams... or to simply sit back and watch.

In partnership with Wirral Borough Council Cultural Services Department and Wirral PCT. Sponsored by University of Liverpool.

"All the world's a stage, and all the men and women merely players..."

As You Like It, Act II, Scene VII (1600)

thereader.co.uk
wirral.gov.uk

22 - 28 September

Sefton Festival of Writing

Various venues

ANNUAL EVENT

Launched last year, this festival hosted a selection of great writers including John Mortimer, Andrew Motion and Michael Marra.

In '08 visitors can look forward to a bigger and better festival with a week of the very best of writing, scriptwriting and poetry experienced through the mediums of readings, performances and film.

There are competitions, book signings and workshops in every form of writing from Haiku to Hollywood scripts.

In celebration of the written word there's also a dance and drama festival for young people entitled: Play Up! – Theatre for Young Imagination.

seftonarts.co.uk
sefton.gov.uk

National Poetry Day

Since 1994 National Poetry Day has engaged millions of people with poetry, ranging from live events to web-based activities for people young and old throughout the country.

Such a variety of poetry is being written and read these days that it was decided to choose a different theme each year to highlight particular poets and styles of poetry.

The day includes residencies, events and participatory activities. In '08, National Poetry Day takes its lead from Liverpool and will embrace and explore the theme of 'work'.

poetrysociety.org.uk

9 - 19 October

Writing at the Bluecoat

the Bluecoat, School Lane

Readings, debates, book launches, performances, workshops and other activities bring writing to the Bluecoat.

Working closely with national publishers, the Bluecoat will host tours by key national and international writers.

Emerging writers will also be part of the programme, which will include a reflection on Liverpool and its global connections, both historical and contemporary.

Amongst writers participating will be those who have a fascination with the impact of the city and of port cities on world culture and world literature.

Expect events to take over every corner of the Bluecoat, with its new arts, eating and drinking spaces, garden and public areas.

thebluecoat.org.uk

November
The Shipping Lines Festival
University of Liverpool, the Bluecoat and others

In Liverpool's maritime past, its shipping lines connected the UK to the rest of the world.

In its present, knowledge, creativity and ideas are the key economic drivers.

The Shipping Lines Festival brings the world of ideas back through the lines of today's greatest writers, featuring Seamus Heaney, Carol Ann Duffy, Jorie Graham, Doris Lessing, Monica Ali, Roger McGough, Philip Pullman (right) and Paul Farley and many others...

This international festival of books, authors and reading welcomes internationally-lauded writers to read, speak and inspire audiences at over 40 interactive and community-based events.

With live readings for adults and children, poetry for both aficionados and beginners, writing competitions for the competitive, and late night talk.

Organised by the University of Liverpool's School of English and The Reader.

liv.ac.uk
thereader.co.uk

7 December
The Penny Readings
St George's Concert Room, William Brown Street

The Reader has hosted this fabulous pre-Christmas literary extravaganza since '03.

Updating the hugely popular readings at this magnificent venue, inspired and given by Charles Dickens in Liverpool in the 1840s, The Penny Readings combine music, dance, laughter, tears and great live readings in one unique Liverpool night out.

With tickets priced at only one penny everyone can afford to give it try.

thereader.co.uk

"The best room in the world for a reading."
Charles Dickens on St George's Concert Room

Also in November: Le Corbusier, Symposium Towards a New Urbanism p 130: Also in December: Labyrinth of Light p 162

Reading for '08:

1 Redburn (1849) by Herman Melville the author of Moby Dick on 19th century Liverpool boiling with fear and poverty. Publisher: Penguin

2 Last and First Men (1930) by Olaf Stapledon sci-fi classic, rated by Arthur C. Clarke as one of the best. Publisher: Dover Publishing

3 The Cruel Sea (1951) by Nicholas Monsarrat on the gruelling life of an Atlantic corvette crew in WWII. Publisher: Weidenfeld Nicolson Illustrated

4 An Awfully Big Adventure (1989) by Beryl Bainbridge draws on her days at the Liverpool Playhouse in Booker-nominated novel. Publisher: Abacus

5 Liverpool wondrous place (2002) by Paul Du Noyer excellent guide charting the city's pop culture. Publisher: Virgin Books

6 Overtaken (2003) by Alexei Sayle a mad vision of a prosperous future Liverpool. Publisher: Sceptre

7 Millions (2004) by Frank Cottrell Boyce children's book about the power of money, set on Merseyside. Publisher: Macmillan Children's Books

8 Liverpool 800: Character, Culture, History (2007) by John Belchem tracing society and culture over eight centuries. Publisher: Liverpool University Press

New Publications for '08

Adrian Henri: Selected and Unpublished
Ed. Catherine Marcangeli

Art in a City by John Willett
1967 classic re-edited

Both Sides of the River by Gladys Mary Coles
Mersey literature through the ages

Irish, Catholic and Scouse by John Belchem
The History of the Liverpool Irish, 1800-1939

The Mersey Sound
Poetry's best-seller, by Henri, McGough and Patten, revised

The Poets Perspective by Gladys Mary Coles
On paintings in the Walker Art Gallery

Featured Author Websites:

Beryl Bainbridge	littlebrown.co.uk
Clive Barker	clivebarker.com
Ramsey Campbell	ramseycampbell.com
Frank Cottrell Boyce	harpercollinschildrens.com
Paul Du Noyer	pauldunoyer.com
Linda Grant	lindagrant.co.uk
Brian Jacques	redwall.org
Astrid Lindgren	astridlindgren.se
Roger McGough	rogermcgough.org.uk
Brian Patten	brianpatten.co.uk
Mal Peet	walkerbooks.co.uk
Willy Russell	willyrussell.com
Alexei Sayle	scepterpublishers.org
Levi Tafari	headlandpublications.co.uk

Literature '08 Calendar

Featured Events:

January
| To 31: | **Astrid Lingren** | liverpoolmuseums.org.uk |
| 24: | **Literate Medicine - Bel Mooney** | lmi.org.uk |

February
| 14: | **Literate Medicine - Rosie Millard** | lmi.org.uk |

March
6-31 Dec:	**Liverpool Reads**	liverpoolreads.com
13:	**Literate Medicine - Raymond Tallis**	lmi.org.uk
14:	**Globalization - The Making of Our World**	sal.org.uk

April
| To May: | **Poetry in the City** | deadgoodpoets.co.uk |
| 7-12: | **Wirral Bookfest** | wirral.gov.uk/libraries |

May
| | **Writing on the Wall** | writingonthewall.org.uk |

July
| 15-26: | **Everyword** | everymanplayhouse.com |

August
| | **Community Shakespeare** | thereader.co.uk |

September
| 19-11 Oct: | **Eric's** | everymanplayhouse.com |
| 22-28: | **Sefton Festival of Writing** | seftonarts.co.uk |

October
1-4:	**National Poetry Day**	poetrysociety.org.uk
9-19:	**Writing at the Bluecoat**	thebluecoat.org.uk
17:	**Burial at Thebes**	liverpoolirishfestival.com

November
| | **Shipping Lines Literary Festival** | liv.ac.uk |
| 3: | **Roscoe Lecture - City of Literature** | ljmu.ac.uk |

December
| 6: | **Literate Medicine - Germaine Greer** | lmi.org.uk |
| 7: | **The Penny Readings** | thereader.co.uk |

Literature '08 Directory

Featured Venues:

Birkenhead Park
Duke Street, Wirral CH41 4HD
0151 606 2000
wirral.gov.uk

Everyman Theatre
13 Hope Street L1 9BH
0151 708 3700
everymanplayhouse.com

Liverpool Medical Institute
Mount Pleasant L3 5SR
0151 709 9125
lmi.org.uk

Picton Reading Room
Liverpool Central Library, William Brown Street L3 8EW
0151 233 5829
liverpool.gov.uk/libraries

St George's Concert Room
William Brown Street L1 1JJ
0151 225 6911
liverpool08.com

the Bluecoat
School Lane L1 3BX
0151 709 5297
thebluecoat.org

Featured Organisations:

Dead Good Poets Society	deadgoodpoets.co.uk
Everyman and Playhouse Theatres	everymanplayhouse.com
Liverpool City Council	liverpool.gov.uk
Liverpool Medical Institution	lmi.org.uk
Liverpool University Press	liverpool-unipress.co.uk
National Museums Liverpool	liverpoolmuseums.org.uk
Sefton MBC	sefton.gov.uk
the Bluecoat	thebluecoat.org.uk
The Poetry Society	poetrysociety.org.uk
The Reader	thereader.co.uk
The Windows Project	windowsproject.co.uk
University of Liverpool	liv.ac.uk
Wirral MBC	wirral.gov.uk
Writing on The Wall	writingonthewall.org.uk

Inspirational

Influential

Take a literary tour of Liverpool by downloading the free 'city of storytellers' guide at **liverpool.gov.uk**

"I fell in love with Liverpool the first time I went there in 1967 as an artist. When I arrived in Liverpool, the first thing that caught my eyes was the beautiful, old elegance of the city by the water. Performing at the Bluecoat is an experience I have never forgotten."

Yoko Ono

THAT SONG, THAT CHORD
THAT MELODY.

romantic

THE BEAT
OF A DIFFERENT
DRUM

radical
crucial

A year of Art

The strength of Liverpool's visual arts played a major role in securing European Capital of Culture '08.

With more galleries and museums than any other city outside London and home to both the John Moores Contemporary Painting Prize and the Liverpool Biennial - the UK's biggest festival of contemporary visual art - the city's arts scene is an all-year affair.

All this is complemented by Tate Liverpool, home of the National Collection of Modern Art in the north of England, and the stunning home for digital and new media, FACT (Foundation for Art and Creative Technology).

There is also a new independent quarter, while internationally-acclaimed work by Antony Gormley on Crosby beach and Richard Wilson with Turning the Place Over have raised the bar for public art.

Liverpool is also experiencing a film boom and after London is the most filmed city in the UK.

In '08 the city will be portrayed on the silver screen fit for the digital age.

And in '08, the arts scene will reach even greater heights with:

· the Bluecoat, Liverpool's oldest building and UK's oldest arts centre, re-opens
· Liverpool John Moores University's new purpose-built Art and Design Academy
· The University of Liverpool's new Victoria Gallery and Museum

Of course, the greatest space is Liverpool itself which in '08 offers its neighbourhoods, parks, roads and transport systems as the canvas for a specially commissioned year-long public art programme.

Like much of the art exhibited this year, expect to see Liverpool in a new light.

8 highlights in 08

November '07 - February '09

Liverpool's Public Art Programme

Various venues

Commissioned from Liverpool Biennial by Liverpool Culture Company for '08

A programme of interventions in city centre and neighbourhood locations includes:

Winter Lights series

Animating the southern, northern and eastern gateways to the city, the Winter Lights series began in winter '06/'07 and started with a commission from Ron Haselden of three light works called 'Animal'. These artworks were re-installed in November '07.

New for '07, French artist, Franck Scurti, created a new series of temporary light works called 'Jackpot' to form visual links in and across Liverpool's neighbourhoods.

These will then be joined by the final Winter Lights commission for '08/'09 resulting in a spectacular series of artists' light works around the city centre periphery.

Pavilions

Specially commissioned for and by their communities, this project allows residents in Vauxhall, Garston and Kensington to show their creativity.

Community engagement is a key element of the '08 public art programme, so three sites were selected to re-introduce the residents to existing underused spaces, with events and cultural exchange programmed throughout '08.

The sites are:

Outside **Rotunda College** in Vauxhall, landscape architect Gross Max transforms this derelict space into an open garden for all residents to use including their very own folly – a building that does not appear on the outside as it does on the inside. **Opens 26 April**.

Edge Hill Station is now a key location for the ongoing programme of activities that Metal Liverpool has planned for Kensington and its residents. The Pavilion installation by Columbian father and son team Luis and Juan Pelaez makes use of the unused cobbled approach to what was the world's first train station. **Opens 2 May**.

Wellington Street School is central to the Garston Cultural Village vision for inviting cultural industries and artists to inhabit and influence cultural-led economic regeneration. Artist Michael Trainor created the Artistic Republic of Garston, making the existing school building into Garston's civic Embassy. **Opens 31 May**.

liverpool08.com
biennial.com
culturalvillage.co.uk
metalculture.com

Throughout '08

Iconic Public Art in the City

Various venues

In '07 Liverpool saw the installation of the most daring piece of public art ever commissioned in the UK.

Turning the Place Over (below) is artist Richard Wilson's most radical intervention into architecture to date, turning a building in Liverpool's city centre literally inside out every minute.

One of Wilson's very rare temporary works, Turning the Place Over colonises Cross Keys House, Moorfields. It runs in daylight hours in summer and 7.30am to 7.30pm in winter.

'08 sees the launch of another major piece of public art, specially commissioned for the city through Liverpool Biennial.

liverpool08.com
biennial.com

Visible Virals:

January - December

Urban Virals

This project entitled 'One Year in Liverpool', by Stockholm artists 'A-APE' explores the habits of Liverpudlians. The project invites the public to feed back facts about themselves. The artworks will then gradually and literally reveal a bigger picture.

liverpool08.com
biennial.com

May - October

Parks Virals

London-based artist Nils Norman will celebrate Liverpool's parks, creating a highly visible artwork which links these hidden gems using the city's transport system.

Supported by Liverpool City Council's Parks and Environment Service and Merseytravel.

liverpool08.com
biennial.com

Until 2 March
Now these days are gone
National Conservation Centre, Whitechapel

This exhibition, from Dundee University, features the photographs of Michael Peto; one of the great photo journalists of the sixties who took hundreds of informal shots of The Beatles as they worked on the set of the 1965 film 'Help'.

liverpoolmuseums.org.uk/conservation

To 27 April '09

DLA Piper Series
The Twentieth Century:
How it looked and how it felt

Tate Liverpool, Albert Dock

Almost 200 works hang across three floors for the largest single display of the Tate Collection ever seen in Liverpool.

The displays tell an interweaving story of modern and contemporary art in two parallel displays, that look at the histories of figurative and abstract art in the 20th century.

Key works include Rodin's The Kiss (above), Picasso's Weeping Woman and Mondrian's Composition with Yellow, Blue and Red.

The ground floor presents solo exhibitions by two major British artists opening with Bridget Riley (September '07 – January '08) followed by Stanley Spencer (February – April '08).

Art on the first floor looks at representational art and the role of the figure within modern and contemporary art.

The second floor traces the journey towards abstraction and explores the variety of abstract art in its many forms.

tate.org.uk/liverpool

Also at Tate Liverpool, don't miss the Turner Prize 07 which runs until 13 January.

To 19 January

John Stezaker

Open Eye, Wood Street

A highlight of the '07 Edinburgh Festival, this is the most substantial exhibition in the UK of John Stezaker's work for many years.

Breathing new life into photographs salvaged from forgotten film archives and old magazines, Stezaker continues the rich history of collage by dissolving the naturalistic to construct a fragmented and dislocated view of contemporary reality.

John Stezaker's work has been influential since the 1970s, when he exhibited with the British Conceptual Art group.

openeye.org.uk

To 16 March

Victorian Visions

Lady Lever Art Gallery, Port Sunlight

This exhibition explores the highly creative world of Victorian photography. The images record the people and places of a very different era. Intense, haunting and romantic.

Victorian Visions is in collaboration with the V&A, London.

liverpoolmuseums.org.uk

25 January - 22 March

Out of Body

Open Eye, Wood Street

Commissioned by Open Eye for '08

A newly commissioned exhibition of photography and moving image.

Out of Body focuses on the relationship between bodily and photographic processes, be it a digital animation of an artist suspended in a 'healing pool', to a video presenting isolated close-ups of body parts which take on a life of their own.

openeye.org.uk

contemporary

challenging

Inspirational

avant garde

the bluecoat

LIVERPOOL EMPIRE THEATRE

The Walker

Another Place

everyman

liverpool biennial

unity theatre

National Conservation Centre

OpenEyeGallery

TATE

Liverpool Playhouse

1 February - 30 March

sk-interfaces

FACT, Wood Street

Commissioned by FACT for '08

EUROPEAN PREMIERE

sk-interfaces launches FACT's programme for '08: Human Futures, exploring materially and metaphorically, the idea of skin as a technological interface.

A programme of exhibitions, events and debates will explore the theme of: My Body, My Mind and My World, with a focus on: Who Am I? Who Are You? And Who Are We?

Debate will centre on the social impact of living in a digital and technologically networked society, how technology affects human experience and awareness, and the role of art and creative technology in shaping human futures.

International curator Jens Hauser presents an exhibition based on years of academic research on issues of biotechnology and the underlying subject of skin.

fact.co.uk

26 February

TWINS
Auditions

by Angie Hiesl and Roland Kaiser

Commissioned by the Bluecoat for '08

Seven pairs of identical adult twins are needed for the climax of the Bluecoat 's live art series for the Liverpool Biennial. Working with the twins from Liverpool and its German twin city of Cologne, will be German choreographer and performance artist, Angie Hiesl, and visual and performance artist Roland Kaiser. Auditions on 26 February. Performances on 21 - 23 November.

thebluecoat.org.uk

29 February - 10 April

The Liverpool Art Prize

Novas Contemporary Urban Centre, Greenland Street

This new annual art competition is for professional artists based in Merseyside.

The exciting shortlist for the '08 prize includes Emma Rodgers (sculptor), The Singh Twins (painters- see p 052), Gareth Kemp (painter), Jayne Lawless (installations), Imogen Stidworthy (audio / visual) and Mary Fitz (photography).

The winner will be announced at the exhibition on 9 March. Prizes awarded by artinliverpool.com and Urban Splash.

liverpoolartprize.com

15 March - 6 April

Now Then

The Bluecoat, School Lane

Commissioned by the Bluecoat for '08

WORLD PREMIERE

Now Then opens the redeveloped Bluecoat presenting newly commissioned work by artists who are either associated with the Bluecoat or are 'rising stars' of the national and international contemporary scene.

Works include:

· A new installation and performance by Yoko Ono - 4 April
· Liverpool-born artist Paul Morrison creates a new drawing on the long wall of the main gallery
· Alec Finlay's 'Specimen Colony' is an installation of brightly painted bird boxes, placed in the gallery, the garden and at the front of the Bluecoat
· Janet Hodgson recreates chase sequences from movies in the empty corridors and spaces, with resulting film to be shown in the gallery
· A heraldic wall sculpture based on coats of arms, made up of thousands of cheap shiny objects, by Hew Locke
· All shows free admission

thebluecoat.org.uk

18 April - 10 August

Art in the Age of Steam

Walker Art Gallery, William Brown Street

This exhibition explores the impact of the railway on the great artists of the 19th and 20th centuries in the city of the world's first commercial passenger line.

With over 100 works including paintings, drawings, prints and photographs, the exhibition features work by Monet, Van Gogh, Manet, Frith and Hopper.

From the social drama of crowds and stations to the conquest of nature by tunnels, cuttings and bridges and the power of the locomotive in motion, the railway changed the way artists saw the world.

Art in the Age of Steam is co-organised by Walker Art Gallery and the Nelson-Atkins Art Museum in Kansas City.

liverpoolmuseums.org.uk

18 April - 8 June

AL and AL

FACT, Wood Street

AL and AL will transport you into a virtual parallel world.

With their spectacular computer-generated videos they radically re-appropriate contemporary pop-culture through an inventive use of celebrity icons, live action performance and animation special effects.

The exhibition features a major new commission developed through the artists' two-year residency at the historically charged Edge Hill Station, in partnership with Metal.

This multiple screen video installation looks at the impact of art and technology on networked societies, responding to Liverpool's unique social, historical and political context.

The new commission in Gallery 1 will be shown alongside two existing works in Gallery 2 originally made for television.

fact.co.uk
metalculture.com

24 May – 2 November

Liverpool Cityscape

By Ben Johnson

Walker Art Gallery, William Brown Street

Commissioned by National Museums Liverpool (NML), Liverpool Culture Company and Professor Phil and Alexis Redmond

This portrait of a city is the painstaking result of an artist using thousands of photographs to depict Liverpool in a detail never seen before.

Liverpool Cityscape, by the contemporary artist and honorary fellow of RIBA, Ben Johnson. The painting will be shown for the first time alongside other panoramas representing 40 years of Johnson's work.

liverpoolmuseums.org.uk

'07 - '08

Singh Twins

St George's Heritage Centre, St John's Lane

Commissioned by Liverpool Culture Company

The acclaimed Singh Twins create two paintings to depict Liverpool's past - for its 800th anniversary in '07 (right) - and its future as a European Capital of Culture.

The '08 painting will depict the city at 'the centre of the creative universe', as a theatrical stage rising from the River Mersey on which the very best in arts, culture and diversity is showcased to the world.

liverpool08.com

30 May - 31 August
Gustav Klimt
Painting, Design and Modern
Life in Vienna 1900

Tate Liverpool, Albert Dock

The first comprehensive exhibition of Gustav Klimt's work ever staged in the UK is an undoubted highlight of '08.

The exhibition focuses on the life and art of one of the world's most influential and revered artists. It explores Klimt's role as the founder and leader of the Viennese Secession, a progressive group of artists and artisans driven by a desire for innovation and renewal and whose vision of the 'total work of art' demanded a new unity between art and society.

The work and philosophy of the Secession embraced art, architecture, fashion, dazzling decorative objects and furniture in the search for identity.

Major paintings and drawings from all stages of Klimt's career will be shown alongside the work of Josef Hoffmann, the architect and designer and a close friend of the artist.

By displaying Klimt's spectacular decorative paintings in settings that recreate his patrons' private residences, the exhibition offers a stunning presentation of his art within the context of one of the highpoints of Viennese modernism.

tate.org.uk/liverpool

Also from 3 - 5 May, Tate Liverpool celebrates its 20th birthday (see page 123).

Jyll Bradley
Fragrant

Various venues

Commissioned by Liverpool Culture Company for '08

International visual artist Jyll Bradley is Artist in Residence within Liverpool Botanical Collection.

One of the largest in UK municipal ownership, the collection was the original vision of one of Liverpool's cultural founding fathers, William Roscoe (1753 - 1831).

In May '08 a garden conceived by Jyll, working in collaboration with Liverpool City Council Parks and Environment Service, will show as part of the Chelsea Flower Show. It will then move to the Tatton Park and Southport Flower Shows (see page 076) and be exhibited at the Bluecoat.

The project will culminate in September with the launch of the artist's book and public art billboard sequence.

Running alongside the Fragrant commission is a participation programme devised by the Bluecoat taking its inspiration from the collection (see page 110).

Developed and produced in collaboration with London Artists Projects. Curated in association with the Bluecoat , in partnership with National Museums Liverpool, Liverpool City Council's Library Service and Parks and Environment Service.

liverpool08.com
thebluecoat.org.uk
jyllbradley.net

19 - 22 June, 10.00am - 6.00pm

Design Show Liverpool

The Crypt, Metropolitan Cathedral of Christ the King, Brownlow Hill

This is a unique opportunity to browse, buy and commission work from over 150 selected designers in contemporary fashion, furniture, garden products clothing and jewellery.

There will be fashion shows, workshops and product presentations running throughout each day of the show.

For family visitors there will be a children's interactive play area.

designshowliverpool.com

28 June - 9 November

Masterpiece Watercolours and Drawings

Lady Lever Art Gallery, Port Sunlight

Some of the finest watercolours and drawings from the Lever collection - many displayed for the first time.

The exhibition includes works by J.M.W. Turner, Edward Burne-Jones and Dante Gabriel Rossetti.

They represent the flowering of the British watercolour school in the 18th century and follow its development through to the early 20th century.

liverpoolmuseums.org.uk

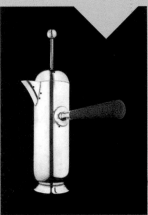

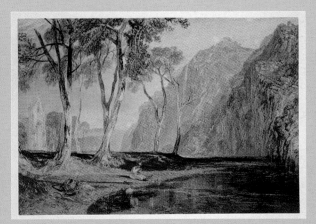

27 June - 31 August

Pipilotti Rist

FACT, Wood Street

Commissioned by FACT for '08

UK PREMIERE

One of Europe's leading contemporary artists Pipilotti Rist (Switzerland), presents a major UK solo exhibition.

Famed for her stunning sculptural video installations that are often presented in unusual locations, the exhibition will traverse the natural to the industrial world.

With a new FACT commission and the UK premiere of - Gravity, Be My Friend - Rist's spectacular and beautiful video installations celebrate the power of self-invention and the creation of new rules for humans living together.

This also completes the third strand of FACT's Human Futures programme, My World, which looks at our relationship to the natural and built environment (see page 50).

fact.co.uk

Also in June: Lord Mayor's Parade p 069 and Once Upon a Time at the Adelphi p 095

10 July - 7 September

Arab Cities
Part of the Liverpool Arabic Arts Festival

the Bluecoat, School Lane and Open Eye Gallery, Wood Street

This thrilling exhibition investigates intersections in art and architecture featuring sculpture, photography, film and installations in the Middle East.

All the works respond to cities such as Baghdad, Beirut, Damascus, Cairo and others.

Presented by the Bluecoat and Open Eye Gallery in collaboration with independent curator November Paynter and Zenith Foundation, London.

thebluecoat.org.uk
openeye.org.uk

Also in July: European Youth Parliament p 127: Also in August: World Firefighters Games p 146

20 September - 30 November

Javier Tellez

A Foundation

WORLD PREMIERE

Fresh from firing a human-cannonball over the US-Mexican border - to explore spatial and mental borders with a group of psychiatric patients - Tellez has been invited to make a new work for Liverpool '08.

In Mexico, the patients and Tellez collectively devised the backdrop, music, costumes, radio and TV announcements and advertising for the happening.

In Liverpool Tellez will work in collaboration with patients from a local psychiatric hospital. Their focus is to explore representations of madness in film specifically concentrating on Lewis Carroll's, Alice in Wonderland (see page 110).

afoundation.org.uk

20 September - 30 November

Phil Collins

A Foundation

Commissioned by Liverpool Culture Company for '08

WORLD PREMIERE

Turner-prize nominee Phil Collins's new film piece is made in collaboration with the people of Liverpool.

Famed for low-budget television and reportage style documentary, Collins creates unpredictable situations with his irreverent use of the camera and intimate engagement with his subjects.

This is a process the Runcorn-born artist describes as 'a cycle of no redemption' - and is as important for his practice as the final presentation in the gallery.

afoundation.org.uk

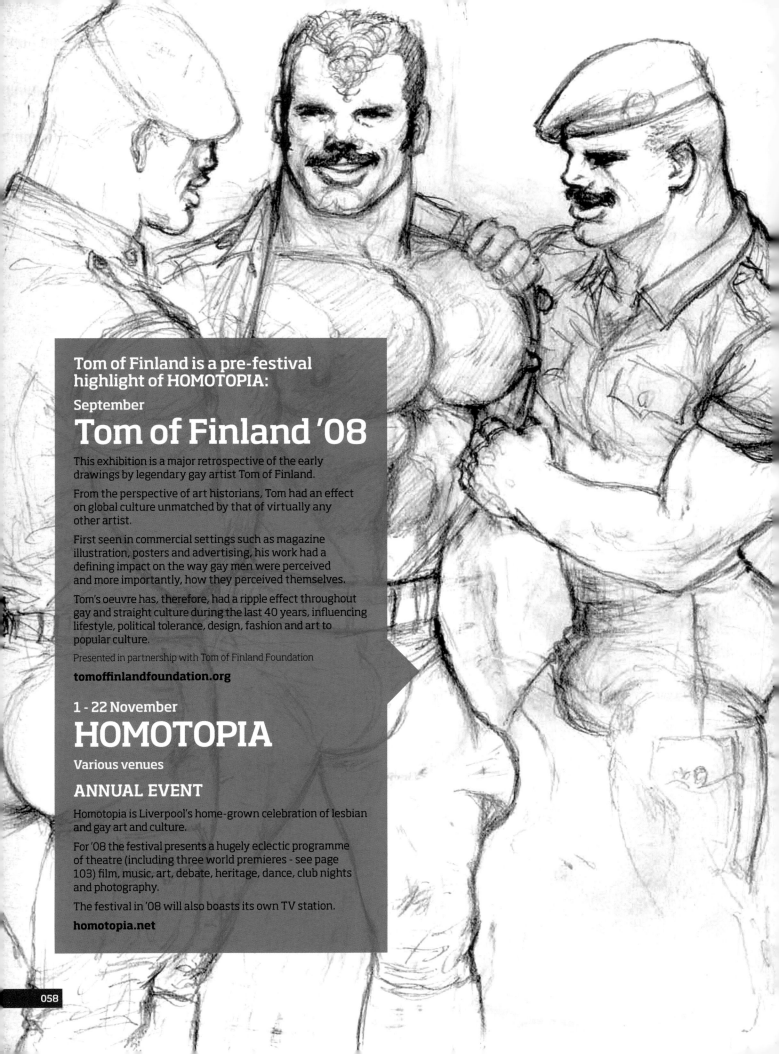

Tom of Finland is a pre-festival highlight of HOMOTOPIA:

September

Tom of Finland '08

This exhibition is a major retrospective of the early drawings by legendary gay artist Tom of Finland.

From the perspective of art historians, Tom had an effect on global culture unmatched by that of virtually any other artist.

First seen in commercial settings such as magazine illustration, posters and advertising, his work had a defining impact on the way gay men were perceived and more importantly, how they perceived themselves.

Tom's oeuvre has, therefore, had a ripple effect throughout gay and straight culture during the last 40 years, influencing lifestyle, political tolerance, design, fashion and art to popular culture.

Presented in partnership with Tom of Finland Foundation

tomoffinlandfoundation.org

1 - 22 November

HOMOTOPIA

Various venues

ANNUAL EVENT

Homotopia is Liverpool's home-grown celebration of lesbian and gay art and culture.

For '08 the festival presents a hugely eclectic programme of theatre (including three world premieres - see page 103) film, music, art, debate, heritage, dance, club nights and photography.

The festival in '08 will also boasts its own TV station.

homotopia.net

20 September - 30 November
Liverpool Biennial

City wide

For '08, **MADE UP**, the fifth edition of Liverpool Biennial, commissions around 40 exciting new artworks by leading international artists of a scale and ambition not to be found elsewhere in the UK.

Many of the new works will be situated in public spaces throughout Liverpool, commissioned in partnership with Tate Liverpool, the Bluecoat , FACT and Open Eye.

Hundreds of the best British artists compete for accolade through the **John Moores 25** Contemporary Painting Prize (20 September - 4 January '09) at the Walker Art Gallery (see John Moores 24 winner below).

Fine art students and recent graduates from across the UK also submit their work for the **Bloomberg New Contemporaries** exhibition.

Additional exhibitions presented through a thriving independent scene will make Liverpool the focus for contemporary arts in Britain, attracting an estimated 500,000 visitors.

biennial.com

Also in October: Power Plant p 080: Also in November: Liverpool Music Week p 028

May - Premiere

All Day and All Night

Liverpool, Newcastle Gateshead, Birmingham and Dublin

Award-winning film-makers Christine Molloy and Joe Lawlor create a feature-length community film in collaboration with partners from Liverpool, Newcastle Gateshead, Birmingham and Dublin.

This project will use a cast of several hundred people for this unique and visually stunning portrait of the four cities and their inhabitants.

Shooting began in October '07, with the finished film expected to be ready for release in March '08 and to then tour the UK and Ireland.

liverpool08.com

July - Broadcast
November - Showcase

High Hopes

By First Take Video Ltd and Sydvest Films

Commissioned by Liverpool Culture Company for '08

This project is a co-production between Liverpool, England and Stavanger, Norway - the EU and non-EU Capitals of Culture in '08.

A documentary series, it follows the lives of 10 teenagers approaching adulthood - each with high hopes for the future - in a tale of these two very different cities.

The films will be aimed at a young audience and artistically will be fast paced, edgy, packed with images, special effects, and music, emotional depth and strong storylines.

Multi-media tie-ins will guarantee content can be geared toward various virtual communities who can design their own viewing experience.

The BAFTA and Prix Italia award-winning Bob Long is the Executive Producer.

first-take.org
sydvestfilm.no

July - August
Movieplex
World cinema in a nutshell

Conceived and co-directed by Ajay Chhabra

Part of Brouhaha International Street Festival and Imagine… Liverpool Children's Festival (see page 075).

Co-commissioned by Liverpool Culture Company for '08

The recently rediscovered, film making dynasty of Shanta Rao Dutt is brought to life by this film, performance and installation piece.

The family's long-lost film making lineage dates back to the end of the 19th century when the Lumiere Brothers first visited India.

Movieplex offers a rare chance to explore some of the resourceful Dutt family's movie making highlights and memorabilia from the past 100 years.

At the sound of the gong, viewers will be ushered through to a plush velvet and gilt encrusted world, as eight-minute films take the Dutt family on a world cinema journey from black and white love story to Technicolor Horror.

Nutkhut are working with Brouhaha and Mersey Film and Video on the creation and presentation of Movieplex.

In partnership with Gem Arts and Culture 10, Newcastle, the Royal National Theatre and BFI on the Southbank, London (tbc).

liverpool08.com

Autumn
Digital Departures

Various venues

Commissioned by Northwest Vision and Media in partnership with Liverpool Culture Company, BBC and the UK Film Council

Writers, producers and directors from the city and across the Northwest were invited to pitch for three feature-length films for '08.

Over 150 film-making teams applied for this dynamic model of micro-budget production that Liverpool aims to export across the world.

The winning films are:

Of Time and The City - Documentary
Writer/Director: Terence Davies

Strastruck - Drama
Writer: Leigh Campbell
Director: Lindy Heyman

Salvage - Horror
Writer: Colin O'Donnell
Director: Lawrence Gough

Guided throughout by industry professionals, each with a budget of £250,000, all three will be developed, shot and post-produced in Liverpool and then premiered in the city.

They will then be distributed nationally and internationally across a variety of digital platforms including the UK's rapidly-expanding Digital Screen Network.

digitaldepartures.co.uk

ICONIC

September
Made in Liverpool

**FACT, Wood Street/BBC Big Screen,
Clayton Square and various venues**

Liverpool Biennial will host an open competition for emerging film-makers to submit and show their work during the prestigious festival period.

Selection will be by panels comprised of local community and youth groups. Successful entrants will be invited to attend a master class by an established film-maker.

Call for submissions will be in spring '08.

biennial.com

19 - 20 September
UNMADE
by The Art Organisation (TAO)

Mello Mello, 40 - 42 Slater Street

Mello Mello will be the focal point for UNMADE, TAO's unique 'non-dependant' Biennial programme.

Unmade is an un-curated and self-organised event where the content will be driven by its participants and defined during the course of the event.

Making the most of the infrastructure developed by TAO across Liverpool and its international network of artists of all disciplines, UNMADE will provide a number of venues, uncovered for the occasion, presenting an alternative remix of artistic manifestations that truly explore the creative wealth inherent to the city.

theartorganisation.co.uk

The River Mersey

melting pot

Adventure

"...from its turbulent past to its bustling present, Liverpool is truly amazing... I've been all over the world looking for excitement and it turns out that the most thrilling town I've ever visited is the one I was born in."

Alexei Sayle

festival city

A year on the Streets

Liverpool's cultural life has a vitality that sees it constantly spilling out onto its streets, parks and public spaces.

The city has always been an arena for world-class outdoor events, embracing great sporting triumphs, international festivals of music and maritime spectaculars.

Now for '08, Liverpool's World Heritage architecture and public spaces become the location for a celebration of outdoor visual art and performance.

New commissions and events that have been specially devised to enhance the annual fixtures will bring colour to the streets and parks.

Artists have been invited from across the globe, to create a potent mix of outdoor cultural activity, ranging from the joyously celebratory Carnival Weekend, to quirky Go Superlambananas and from the magic of the Liverpool's Streets Ahead weekend through to the city's public art programme.

Expect plenty of performance and spectacle unique to a remarkable city.

8 highlights in 08

10 February

Chinese New Year Celebrations

Chinatown, Nelson Street

Liverpool is home to one of the oldest Chinese communities in Europe. Chinese New Year is celebrated at the Chinese Arch on Nelson Street and '08 is the Year of the Rat.

Prepare to be mesmerised by dancing dragons, unicorns and lions, special firecracker performances and Tai Chi demonstrations. It is also a great opportunity to enjoy Chinese food and traditional New Year's delicacies.

liverpool08.com

17 - 18 May

HUB Festival

Otterspool Park, Otterspool Drive

ANNUAL EVENT

One of Britain's best, free urban youth festivals, jam-packed with live music and competitions, featuring legends in BMX, skate boarding, break-dancing and graffiti art.

liverpool08.com

24 - 26 May

Liverpool Streets Ahead

St George's Plateau and city centre

Presented by M.I.A.

Commissioned by Liverpool Culture Company for '08

Liverpool will be awash with fantastic street theatre, music, dance, puppets, both shows and spectacle, featuring leading artists from all over the world.

With shows on every corner, roaming acts along the streets, surprises in the squares and shop windows, performers hanging 60 feet above your head, the best of European street arts of the past decade are revealed. Streets Ahead will be a high energy weekend of delights culminating on Bank Holiday Monday evening when the festival is handed over to you, the audience, to 'play the city'.

liverpool08.com
streetsahead.org.uk

 Also in March: St David's Day Concert p 017: Also in April: The Shankly Show p 094

7 June, start 1.00pm

Lord Mayor's Parade

Liverpool city centre

ANNUAL EVENT

Presented by Liverpool Culture Company for '08

Specially enhanced for '08, Liverpool's Walk the Plank and the Liverpool Lantern Company collaborate to add amazing images, fantastic music and colourful costumes to the parade.

Artists will be working with community groups and local businesses to create spectacular floats, which are wheeled, pushed or pulled through the streets, while carnival bands and street performance spill out from the parade route to animate the whole city.

Featured floats will include those made by and with people from the Caribbean Centre, the Liverpool Arabic Arts Festival, Homotopia, Tara Park Travellers Community, the Hindu Cultural Organisation, the Chinese community and many, many more.

liverpool08.com

7 - 8 June, 11.00am - 4.00pm

Kites over the Mersey

International Kite Festival

New Brighton promenade, Wirral

ANNUAL EVENT

The UK's biggest international kite festival features champion stunt flyers and massive show kites in all sorts of imaginative designs.

As well as kite flying, there will be workshops for children and, if they bring their teddy bear along, they can enter into the teddy drop when they will be parachuted into the main arena from a static kite!

wirral.gov.uk

8 June, 11.00am – 5.00pm

The Green Fayre

Court Hey Park, Roby Road, Huyton

ANNUAL EVENT

Each year this event promotes World Environment Day with a wealth of information on green issues, from solar power to composting, recycling to climate change.

The event also features local craft and food stalls, recycled art and craft workshops, live music, circus show and a dedicated early years area too.

The National Wildflower Centre, based in the park, will also open its doors free of charge for the day. Visitors are encouraged to use public transport to attend the event.

The Green Fayre is organised by Knowsley Council, in partnership with The National Wildflower Centre and Liverpool Culture Company.

knowsley.gov.uk
nwc.org.uk

Also in May: Gustav Klimt exhibition p 053: Also in June: Liverpool Sound p 021

changing

wonderously diverse

16 June - 25 August

Go Superlambananas

City wide

Commissioned by Liverpool Culture Company for '08

Liverpool will be transformed by this open-air, free-to-view, mass public appeal art event.

Up to 100, 180cm-tall Superlambananas, one of Liverpool's most iconic and best-loved pieces of public art - originally, created by Taro Chiezo for Arts Transpennine in 1998 - will be painted, decorated and adorned by local and regional artists, community groups and celebrities.

The Go Superlambanana sculpture has been specially designed to act as a 3-D canvas to showcase the creativity of Liverpool.

After the event many of the Superlambananas will be sold at a charity auction with a significant percentage of the proceeds going to local charities.

**liverpool08.com
wildinart.com**

29 June

Liverpool Open Gardens

The Palm House, Sefton Park and other venues

Two superb private gardens previously unseen by the public, plus 90 city allotments, will open their gates for the first time to celebrate '08.

One show will be the Toxteth garden of the University of Liverpool's Vice-Chancellor, and the new garden of one of Liverpool's old merchant houses overlooking Sefton Park, designed by Jeremy Nicholls.

Allotments in Sefton Park will offer inspiration to other city gardeners while the Palm House (right) will provide afternoon teas for garden visitors, and stalls selling rare and unusual plants.

Supporting the National Garden Scheme.

palmhouse.org.uk
ngs.org.uk

July - August

Hope Street Ltd Public Art Programme

Speke and Garston

Commissioned by Hope Street Ltd for '08

This is an eight-week site-specific project to create a piece of public art sited in the vicinity of Liverpool John Lennon Airport.

Four designs will be created entirely from the input of the public. Models will be displayed locally and the community will vote on which should go forward for production.

The final artwork will be sited where it can be seen by local residents and visitors, as they fly into the city.

hope-street.org

5 - 6 July
St Helens Festival

Sherdley Park, Marshalls Cross Road, Sutton

ANNUAL EVENT

In '08, this free festival plays host to a high action main arena, music stage, arts and culture, food festival, craft and flowers, fun fair, children's entertainment and much more.

In the surroundings of 200 acres of parkland, businesses, community groups, schools, voluntary groups, charities, artists, performers and more showcase their work.

festival.sthelens.gov.uk

12 - 13 July
Halton Youth Culture Festival

Halton Stadium, Widnes

ANNUAL EVENT

An invitation for all young people to come and see the best of youth culture on Merseyside. The twin towns of the region will also be invited to send their young people for what is going to be a weekend to remember.

halton.gov.uk

12 - 13 July
The Wirral Show

New Brighton

ANNUAL EVENT

One of the biggest free weekend shows in England, now in its 32nd year, boasts a full programme of air and land-based entertainment, including one of the largest outdoor funfairs in the country.

Also featured are military shows, aircraft displays, stunt shows, musical marvels and special amusements for children.

wirralshow.com

Also in July: Liverpool Arabic Arts Festival p 056 and Clipper '07/'08 Race Finish p 141

1 - 3 August

Carnival Weekend

Highlights include:

2 August

Brouhaha International Festival Parade and Princes Park Festival

Liverpool City Centre and Princes Park

The region's largest multi-cultural parade sees the final part of a four-year programme 'Crossing Waters', depicting the story of Liverpool's participation in the transatlantic slave trade.

Through the costume designs of award-winning artist Ray Mahabir, the fourth installment 'Viey La Cou, theatre of the streets' will be the largest single body of carnival arts work in the UK.

Participating groups and communities will undertake arts workshops with some of the world's finest musicians, dancers, costume makers, puppeteers and stilt walkers.

brouhaha.uk.com

2 August

Samba School

The Samba School is bringing a Rio-style carnival parade to the streets of Liverpool for '08.

Groups from across Liverpool, the UK, Europe and Brazil will parade and take centre stage in a glittering sea of colour, magical floats, costumes, theatre and live music.

A year in the making, the parade will end in the independent district with an outdoor music festival until the early hours.

carnival.org.uk

1 - 10 August
Imagine ...

St George's Hall, William Brown Street and St John's Gardens

Ten days of performances and activities that invite children and young people to use their imagination and creativity.

These 10 days feature: The Emperor and the Tiger and Sensazione, building towards the Liverpool Children's Festival.

6 - 10 August
Sensazione

St George's Plateau, Lime Street

Free to roam, the attractions of this theatrical fairground need your physical energy, enthusiasm and imagination.

Time Circus and Laika seek interaction between performers and spectators and believe that theatre can pull down boundaries between them.

Co-produced by Crying Out Loud. Sensazione by Time Circus and Laika supported by CC MUZE & Circo Paradiso, Theaterfestival Boulevard, Nationale Loterij.

liverpool08.com

1 August
The Emperor and the Tiger

Presented by Liverpool Culture Company for '08

Walk the Plank and Kinetika join forces with Brouhaha and local performers to present a beautiful folk story. As a giant tiger paces through the park, fire illuminates costumed carnival dancers and drummers, and firework effects light up the forest. The greedy Emperor wants his taxes, and the people must pay. An original soundtrack and magical special effects animate this colourful tale of the Emperor, the Wise Man, and the Guardian of the Jungle - before the firework finale lights up the skies.

Originally commissioned by the London Borough of Tower Hamlets.

liverpool08.com

8 August
Liverpool Children's Festival
ANNUAL EVENT

An imaginary city mysteriously appears to transform Liverpool's historical cultural quarter. Featuring a host of performances and workshops, this annual festival was the original idea of Liverpool's Young Culture Action Group, when Liverpool was bidding to be European Capital of Culture. Through performance and visual art activities the festival celebrates the culturally diverse heritage of Liverpool. In '08, expect several surprises that will stretch and stimulate your imagination.

Supported by The Greenhouse Project, Liverpool Culture Company and The Cultures of Childhood Network.

liverpool08.com

10 August, 11.00am – 5.00pm

Knowsley Flower Show

Court Hey Park, Roby Road, Huyton

ANNUAL EVENT

The largest free horticultural show in the Northwest.

The show offers experienced gardeners and novices the opportunity to enter more than 100 classes, ranging from potted plants, vegetables and fruit to floral art.

Its Floral and Plant Society marquees feature more than 400 exhibits with craft and plant displays to enjoy as well.

Other entertainment includes falconry, dog display team as well as live music and theatre. The Youth Arts Friendship Field also features live music, dance and craft activities.

knowsleyflowershow.com

21 – 24 August

Southport Flower Show

Victoria Park, Rotten Row

ANNUAL EVENT

Now in its 79th year, Britain's largest independent flower show will be themed around Liverpool '08, celebrating the heritage, architecture, culture and artists of this great city.

Visitors can expect to see spectacular show gardens including Jyll Bradley's Fragrant Liverpool (see page 054), water features and one million beautiful blooms. They can also chat to gardening experts, browse the arts and crafts or watch cookery demonstrations by celebrity chefs.

There is live music, arena entertainment and the new Kidz Kr8, a marquee dedicated to learning about the environment, healthy eating, physical development and outdoor fun.

Children under 16 go free when accompanied by a paying adult.

southportflowershow.co.uk

6 – 7 September, 9.00am – 6.00pm

Southport Airshow

Southport Seafront

ANNUAL EVENT

The region's largest air show features a superb mix of military, civilian and historic aircraft.

Highlights over recent years have included the Red Arrows Display Team, the Typhoon (Eurofighter), Harrier Jump Jets, Tornados, Jaguars as well as helicopters, parachute display teams and the Battle of Britain Memorial Flight.

The air show village contains interactive attractions, static aircraft, military vehicles, assault course, stalls, children's rides and much more.

sefton.gov.uk
militaryairshows.co.uk

21 September
The Market of Optimism

Presented by Hope Street Limited as part of Hope Street Feast

ANNUAL EVENT

Taking the Hope Street Feast and the architecture of Hope Street as its inspiration, a group of national and international artists will animate Hope Street and its buildings. The performances and animations will take place over a week, with one or two happenings each day, culminating on the final day with all the animations and performances and a few finale surprises.

This will incorporate up to 20 ridiculous market stalls, specially invented street musicians, roof top hawkers, flapping carpets, singers and vendors of every description. Punters will be awarded 100 'neuros' as they enter at either end of Hope Street. They will be free to spend them however they wish. Every 'product' would be inspirational or the answer to a wish however small. Each stall and product will be designed as a unique artistic element.

These performances will incorporate lots of original music and songwriting/inventive sound installation/much design, performance and sculpture. The whole experience would be a cacophonous hurly burly somewhere between the world of 'Oliver!' and Marrakech.

hope-street.org
hopestreetfeast.com

19 - 21 September
British Musical Fireworks Championships

Kings Gardens, Southport

ANNUAL EVENT

Six of the country's best fireworks display companies go head-to-head over three nights to see who will hold this prestigious title for the next 12 months.

Visitors are advised to arrive early as there is some great entertainment prior to the main event.

Each night two companies will provide an incredible festival of sound and light as they choreograph their displays to a music programme of their choice.

With '08 being the competition's 10th anniversary expect a special 'Champion of Champions' event.

visitsouthport.com

Also in September: Berliner Philharmoniker p 024 and Sefton Festival of Writing p 039

4 - 7 September

Strictly Awesome

All over Liverpool

WORLD PREMIERE

Produced by Artichoke
Commissioned by Liverpool Culture Company for '08

In May '06 something incredible happened in London. For four days the city stopped in its tracks and marvelled at the sight of a gigantic wooden elephant, and a little-girl giant in a green dress.

A million people jammed the streets, astonished at the scale and beauty of the spectacular Sultan's Elephant.

Now Artichoke, the company that brought that event to London, is planning a magical new show, created specially for Liverpool '08.

The precise details are a closely-guarded secret, but what's certain is that it will be huge in scale and utterly unlike anything seen in Liverpool before: an unforgettable piece of live theatre, played out against the landmarks of a great city.

Will you find it? Register for updates and you just might.

willyoufindit.co.uk

078

27 - 28 September

Vintage Fair
and Organ Rally

Victoria Park, Widnes

The major free vintage event in the North of England.

Over 40,000 visits in 2005 to see over 50 fairground organs and 200 vintage attractions including classic cars, motorbike and traction engines. A great free family day out.

halton.gov.uk

8 - 12 October

Power Plant

Walled Gardens, Calderstones Park, Menlove Avenue

Power Plant is a night-time trail of sound and light installations creating a magical, audio-visual journey.

Approaches include video and electronic sound to modifications of old gramophones, moving speakers, sound sources hidden in the undergrowth, circular saw blades played like gongs and balloons filled with tuned harmonicas that whisper an eerie melancholic requiem.

Artists include Mark Anderson, Anne Bean, Kirsten Reynolds and Jony Easterby. Produced by Simon Chatterton for Arts Council England's Contemporary Music Network.

Originally commissioned by Oxford Contemporary Music and University of Oxford Botanic Garden.

powerplant.org.uk

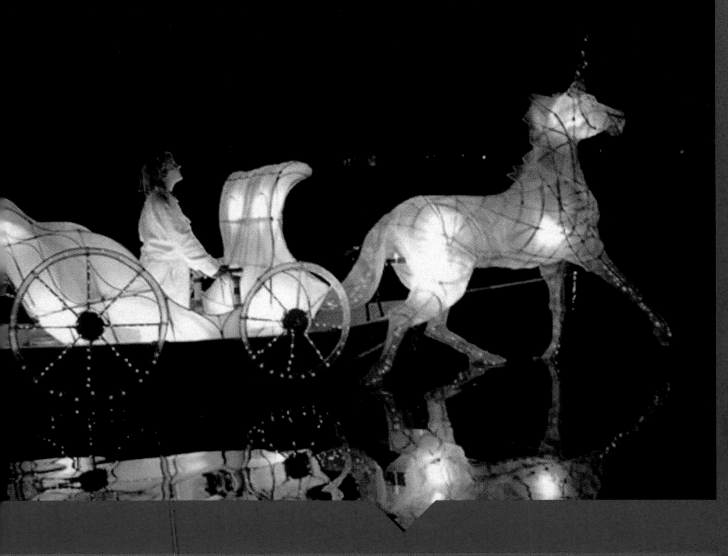

31 October

Halloween Lantern Parade

Presented by Liverpool
Lantern Company

Sefton Park, Croxteth Drive

ANNUAL EVENT

A highlight of the Liverpool calendar, this parade involves
15 partner organisations and over 20 community groups.

In '08 the Halloween lantern carnival incorporates a kinetic
lantern, water and fire festival with the theme of 'Phoenix
Rising' and a cast of over 200 performers, pyrotechnicians
and musicians in an extraordinary celebratory uprising.

liverpoollanterncompany.co.uk
liverpool08.com

Ends Autumn

Water, Water Everywhere and Not a Drop to Drink

By Jump Ship Rat, featuring Jacques Chauchat and Ben Parry

Various waterfront venues

A Liverpool Commission

Commissioned by Liverpool Culture Company for '08

The importance of water to survival in the 21st century and Liverpool's maritime history will be explored through a giant wind and water-powered environmental sculpture.

The hull of a 60ft steel boat forms the armature for an intricate water channelling system; using wind and hydro energy alongside traditional methods such as Archimedes screw; water is pumped from the dock in perpetual motion - water rises, falls and flows around the boat, flushing, pouring and splashing in a spectacle of movement and colour.

Inspired by the desperation in Samuel Coleridge's 'The Rime of the Ancient Mariner', this work reinterprets the world water crisis from global warming to hydrological poverty.

The animation of colour and form through water and wind articulates our manipulation of nature, but recognises the great challenge of our century: to develop alternative and intuitive ways of living that save the planet for future generations.

jumpshiprat.org
liverpool08.com

Throughout '08:

The Line

By Collision

A Liverpool Commission

Commissioned by Liverpool Culture Company for '08

The Line is a large-scale line of choreography, which brings more than 100 different people together to create a line that makes some unlikely appearances.

Emerging out of the crowd, everywhere from football pitches to shopping parades, audiences will be able to stand and wait to see The Line as an 'event' or just 'happen' upon it whilst strolling about the streets, out and about visiting, or shopping in the city.

"The line of life, the crossing of borders, the link, the holding of hands, crossing rivers, re-uniting, connecting different communities and building bridges." Lisi Perry, Director of Collision

collisiondance.co.uk

GATEWAY TO THE WORLD

In England, but not of it

SEA SHANTIES AND SALTY SEA DOGS

TALL SHIPS

Also in November: Liverpool is Burning p 103: Also in December: Choir of the Year p 031

A year on Stage

Embedded in Liverpool is a spirit that infuses the very fabric of life and finds expression in a thriving drama and dance culture.

Blessed with fantastic venues from The Empire Theatre, The Everyman and Playhouse and Philharmonic Hall to the Bluecoat, the city has consistently been a catalyst for brilliant performance.

Talent is nurtured in no less than 10 performing arts colleges and at least 43 courses, as well as theatres like the Everyman and unity.

In '08, showcases such as British Dance Edition provide a springboard for emerging talent, as will special commissions such as Liverpool is Burning, Babul and the Blue Bear, Once Upon a Time at the Adelphi and Eric's.

This is complemented by an all-year programme of popular theatre and dance, with regular visits from companies such as the English National Ballet and Welsh National Opera.

Then there's the repertory theatre that has been the backbone of the city's arts for decades with its cutting-edge comedy, the originality of its writing and its provocative drama.

And with the community at the heart there will be a play for the people.

All of this - and much, much more - will be realised in a special year for the performing arts.

8 highlights in

08

To 26 January
Blood Brothers

By Willy Russell

Empire Theatre, Lime Street

Hailed by the critics as one of the best musicals of all time, Liverpool's multi, award-winning Blood Brothers is celebrating its 25th year in '08.

Set in Willy Russell's native Liverpool, it tells the captivating tale of twin boys, separated at birth only to be re-united by a twist of fate and a mother's haunting secret.

This silver anniversary run includes special New Year's Eve and New Year's Day performances.

"Most Popular British Musical." New York Times

clearchannel.com

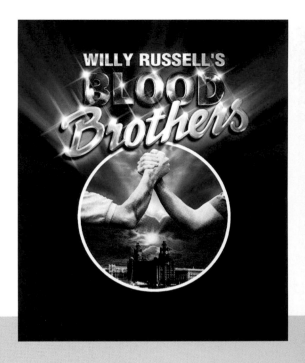

25 January - 16 February
3 Sisters on Hope Street

By Diane Samuels and Tracy-Ann Oberman, after Chekhov

Everyman Theatre, Hope Street

Lindsay Posner, director

WORLD PREMIERE

Commissioned by Liverpool Everyman and Playhouse and Hampstead Theatre for '08

Liverpool, 1946, stranded after the death of their father, sisters Gertie, May and Rita share their crowded home with their brother Arnold and his wife, May's pedantic husband, a demanding aunt and a cynical lodger.

As the young women search for meaning and hope amidst the upheaval of their post-war world, daily life and complications continue to tighten their hold on them.

This vibrant take on Chekhov's classic relocates the story from Russia to Liverpool's Jewish community of 1946-8.

It also unites the talents of Diane Samuels (Kindertransport) and celebrated actress Tracy-Ann Oberman to create a powerful and witty new drama.

everymanplayhouse.co.uk

31 January - 2 February, 11.00am - 11.00pm

British Dance Edition

Empire Theatre, Lime Street and various venues

One of the foremost events in the UK dance calendar attracts hundreds of national and international dance promoters, in search of the latest talent and ideas.

Liverpool's theatres and alternative spaces host an eclectic programme of diverse and contemporary dance performance; profiling new and emerging work, alongside more well known and established companies.

Two gala shows are open to the public at the Liverpool Empire on 31 January and 2 February. These feature stunning choreography from a unique collection of artists:

Programme 1: Russel Maliphant Company, Henri Oguike Dance Company, Scottish Dance Theatre.

Programme 2: Shobaba Jeyasingh Dance Company, Hofesh Shechter, Richard Alston Dance Company.

bde2008.co.uk

5 - 9 February

Anima

by Momentum

unitytheatre, Hope Place

WORLD PREMIERE

A Liverpool Commission

Commissioned by Liverpool Culture Company for '08

Based on dreams and the subconscious life, Anima is the final part of a trilogy in a quest for understanding the human essence.

Personal statements, dreams and ideas merge with universal and mythical stories to produce a piece of physical theatre that explores how reality and our dream world affect each other, and experiments with the conflict and the unity within each of us.

Anima is highly visual and experiments with innovative lighting design, projection, animation and live music from the experienced creative team.

momentum.com
unitytheatreliverpool.co.uk

1 - 15 March
LEAP Festival
ANNUAL EVENT

Now in its 16th year, Merseyside's only annual dance festival profiles innovative works from national and international companies as well as community groups and local artists.

leap08.co.uk

A highlight of '08 will be:

7 - 8 March
Akram Khan - bahok
with the National Ballet of China

Liverpool Playhouse, Williamson Square

UK PREMIERE

Co-produced by Liverpool Culture Company for '08 with Merseyside Dance Initiative and Akram Khan Company

bahok is the long-awaited new group choreography by Akram Khan, based on the tale of Babel.

Working with long-time collaborators, acclaimed writer Hanif Kurieshi, multi award-winning composer Nitin Sawhney, Khan will also be collaborating with The National Ballet of China for the piece.

The dancers from different cultures, traditions and dance backgrounds: Chinese, Korean, Indian, South African and Spanish, want to create a utopian project speaking both with their bodies and tongues.

They meet in one of this globalised world's transit zones and try to communicate, to share 'the things they carry with them', their experiences, their memories of their original homes, the dreams and aspirations that made them move. They are carriers. They are bahok.

"For nomads, home is not an address, home is what they carry with them."

John Berger, Hold Everything Dear

akramkhancompany.net
merseysidedance.co.uk

The Walker

everyman

liverpool biennial

unity theatre

National Conservation Centre

RISKY

FACT

Also in March: The Long Walk p 017 and Carnival Olympiad Seminar p 122

Liverpool Playhouse

FACT

DRAMA

24 April
The Shankly Show
by Footballing Legends Ltd

**Liverpool Olympia, West Derby Road
and on tour at selected venues**

WORLD PREMIERE
A Liverpool Commission

Commissioned by Liverpool Culture Company for '08

35 years since Liverpool FC last won the English First Division under the legendary Bill Shankly, comes a play about one man and his perpetual influence on a city, the world of sport and popular culture.

One actor, 45 minutes each way - first half in black and white, with half-time oranges; then second half in colour - a live television event in a theatre.

This new piece of interactive, multi-media theatre, projects a cross between a personal audience with Shankly, the legend and the myth, and an in-depth documentary about Liverpool.

Created by Andrew Sherlock and Brian Machin, with help from fans, LFC and ITV Granada.

"I was only in the game for the love of football - and I wanted to bring back happiness to the people of Liverpool."

Bill Shankly

footballinglegends.com

April
Nirumpama and Rajenda

Commissioned by Milapfest for '08

Leading dancer/choreographers of India, Nirumpama and Rajendra are world-renowned for their dynamic, captivating, and colourful dances.

Here they present innovative new productions based in the beautiful and graceful Indian dance forms of Kathak and Bharatanatyam.

milapfest.com

28 May - 8 June

Liverpool Comedy Festival

Various venues

ANNUAL EVENT

Established in '02 as part of the city's '08 bid, this festival has grown to attract some of the best names in comedy.

With comic plays, comedy workshops, laughter therapy, one-man shows and stand-up comedy nights, this festival tries to cover everything that is funny.

Last year it attracted over 18,000 people and along with critical acclaim, as well as legendary Liverpool wit from the audiences, here's to more of the same this year.

"Simply a who's who of comedy's intelligent talent." Metro

liverpoolcomedyfestival.co.uk

28 June - 19 July

Once Upon a Time at the Adelphi

A new musical by Phil Willmott

Liverpool Playhouse, Williamson Square

WORLD PREMIERE

Presented by Liverpool Everyman and Playhouse

Writer/Director Phil Willmott spent a year gathering stories about the Adelphi before choosing the meeting of movie stars and 1930s Liverpool as this musical's setting.

Here the glitz and glamour of Hollywood pour off the luxury liners for their first taste of England; a night in the city's most fashionable hotel.

Amidst the chaos and decadence, no-nonsense Alice from reception has fallen for the dashing Thompson from accounts - but fate, Hollywood, two world wars and a dizzying array of staff and guests intervene in an epic Liverpool love story spanning 60 years.

"Irresistibly amusing... tunes by the writer -director echo the style of Old Broadway."

The Independent on Sunday on 'Around the World in Eighty Days' by Phil Willmott

everymanplayhouse.com

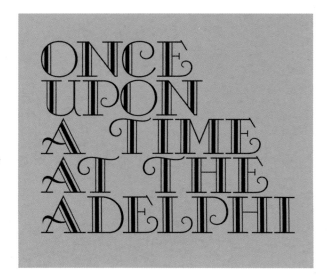

fresh
real
what rules!
SEMINAL
AN EVER-CHANGING
CANVAS

27 July - 2 August
Contacting the World
Various venues

Hundreds of young theatre-makers across the world take part in an extraordinary process of international, creative exchange.

In October '07, 150 young people (aged 13-30) from 10 different countries were twinned for 10 months to share their lives, hopes, passions and dreams.

In July '08, 12 new theatre performances, created as a result of this unique collaboration, will be premiered together in Liverpool.

This work is presented alongside a programme of public workshops, discussions (see page 121), late night music and street performances.

This production is brought to Liverpool by Contact - a pioneering, award-winning theatre venue in Manchester.

contact-theatre.org
liverpool08.com

Autumn

Babul and the Blue Bear

by 20 Stories High

WORLD PREMIERE

A Liverpool Commission

Commissioned by Liverpool Culture Company for '08

Once upon a grime, in a land not so far away, lived a young man called Benny. He existed in limbo in outer space with his only friend Blue Bear for company.

One day something unexpected happened... Benny looked down, upon the earth and saw himself hooked up to a life-support machine.

Babul and the Blue Bear explores the themes of cultural identity, divided loyalties, racial tension and a sense of belonging in a multi-cultural Britain.

With the help of Bob Frith from Horse and Bamboo, this new company brings the worlds of hip-hop and theatre, Heavy Grime music, spoken word, body-popping, mask and puppetry together in an exhilarating way.

The play is suitable for ages 13+

20storieshigh.org.uk

4 - 8 September
International DaDa Fest
Various venues

ANNUAL EVENT

Disabled and Deaf artists from every continent present a programme that reflects the very best in their fields.

The intention is to develop a global voice and cultural identity and ensure that the learning from the festival and its conference is preserved and analysed as well as ensuring a lasting legacy.

nwdaf.co.uk

Autumn
When We Dead Awaken
By Henrik Ibsen

In collaboration with Riksteatern and Vasterbottensteatern of Sweden

unitytheatre, Hope Place

UK PREMIERE

The final dramatic work from one of Scandinavia's greatest playwrights is brought to the stage under the direction of Josette Bushell-Mingo (left).

Josette, who created the role of Rafiki in the UK premiere of the Lion King, is a patron of unitytheatre and a co-founder of PUSH, the major festival celebrating contemporary Black arts and Black artists.

Josette is currently artistic director of Tyst Teater, which is part of the Riksteatern's national touring programme.

Throughout '08 unity will be presenting several premieres alongside the work of the best local, national and international touring companies.

In particular it will be promoting, throughout June and July, as part of its annual Splatterfest programme of children's theatre, companies from Italy, Denmark and Canada.

unitytheatreliverpool.co.uk

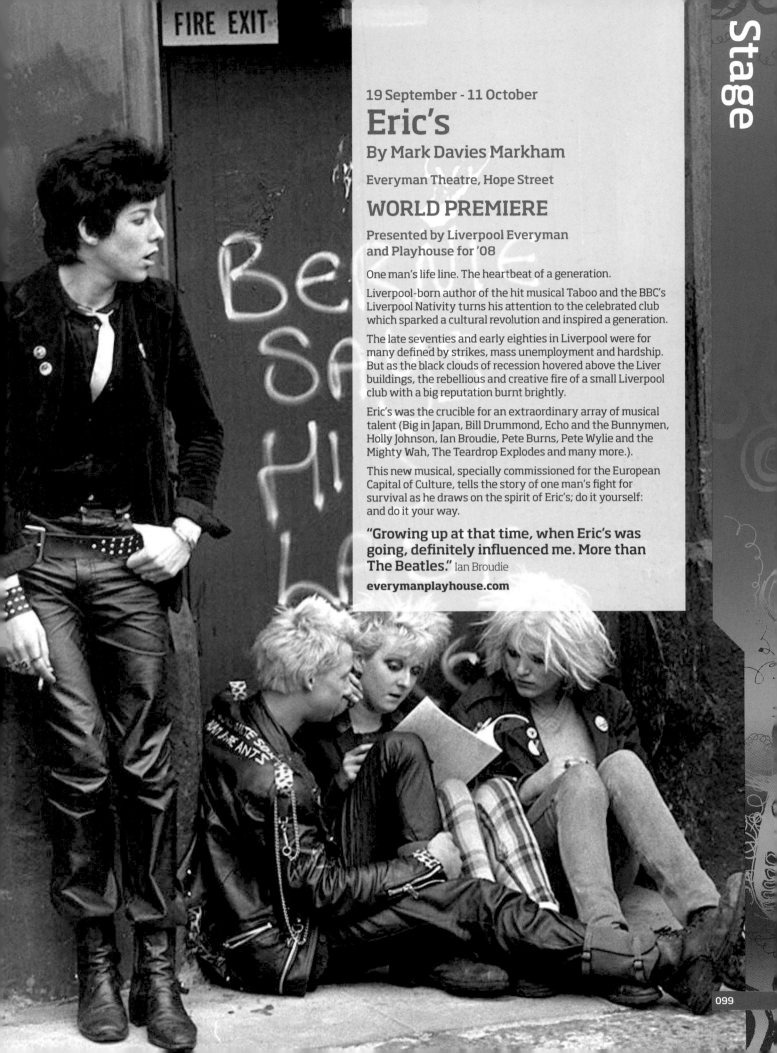

FIRE EXIT

19 September - 11 October

Eric's

By Mark Davies Markham

Everyman Theatre, Hope Street

WORLD PREMIERE

Presented by Liverpool Everyman and Playhouse for '08

One man's life line. The heartbeat of a generation.

Liverpool-born author of the hit musical Taboo and the BBC's Liverpool Nativity turns his attention to the celebrated club which sparked a cultural revolution and inspired a generation.

The late seventies and early eighties in Liverpool were for many defined by strikes, mass unemployment and hardship. But as the black clouds of recession hovered above the Liver buildings, the rebellious and creative fire of a small Liverpool club with a big reputation burnt brightly.

Eric's was the crucible for an extraordinary array of musical talent (Big in Japan, Bill Drummond, Echo and the Bunnymen, Holly Johnson, Ian Broudie, Pete Burns, Pete Wylie and the Mighty Wah, The Teardrop Explodes and many more.).

This new musical, specially commissioned for the European Capital of Culture, tells the story of one man's fight for survival as he draws on the spirit of Eric's; do it yourself: and do it your way.

"Growing up at that time, when Eric's was going, definitely influenced me. More than The Beatles." Ian Broudie

everymanplayhouse.com

099

September

Play for the People

Royal Court Liverpool, Queen Square

Royal Court Liverpool will be working with the Liverpool ECHO, the city's evening newspaper, to find the public's favourite Liverpool play of the last 50 years.

Once a shortlist has been drawn up by journalists and theatre management, the public will be invited to vote for a play to fill a four-week slot at Royal Court Liverpool.

Polls will open in spring '08.

**icliverpool.co.uk
royalcourtliverpool.co.uk**

11 - 14 October

Fiesta Latina

Various venues

ANNUAL EVENT

The UK's only Latin-American Festival creates four vibrant days of dance, drama, music and other activities from top international artists.

A masquerade (multi-media/dance), a family day, a series of workshops and seminars (with Latin American artists presenting their work and delivering top quality workshops and master classes) make for an unforgettable celebration.

fiesta-latina.co.uk

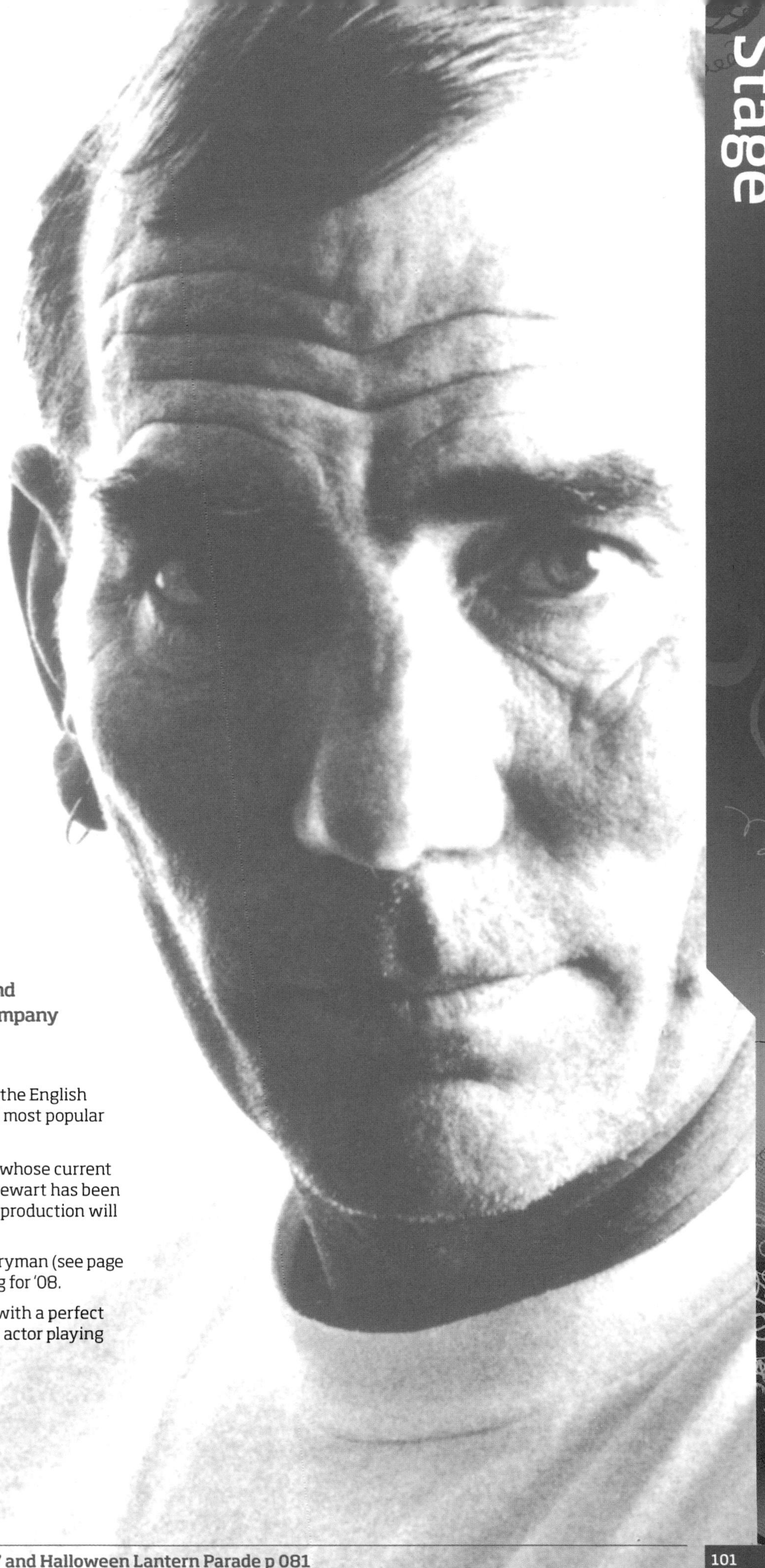

30 October - 29 November

Pete Postlethwaite is

King Lear

by William Shakespeare

Everyman Theatre, Hope Street

Presented by Liverpool Everyman and Playhouse and Headlong Theatre Company

Rupert Goold, director

Perhaps the greatest play ever written in the English language starring one of the greatest and most popular actors of our time.

Under the eye of an exceptional director, whose current production of Macbeth starring Patrick Stewart has been hailed by audiences and critics alike, this production will be the climax of their theatrical year.

Pete began his theatrical career at the Everyman (see page 086) and makes an emotional homecoming for '08.

This is an extraordinary theatrical event with a perfect cocktail of artistic team, text, and leading actor playing the ultimate role in the theatrical canon.

everymanplayhouse.com

Also in October: Burial at Thebes p 027 and Halloween Lantern Parade p 081

Brand New World
By Positive Impact

Royal Court Liverpool, Queen Square

To celebrate '08 comes an urban contemporary musical based on the story of Aladdin.

This theatrical production by Liverpool's leading multi-ethnic drama groups, will combine original songs, show-stopping dance routines and soulful singing.

liverpool08.com

25 - 29 November

Sleeping Beauty
by English National Ballet

Liverpool Empire, Lime Street

With over 50 years of association with Liverpool and its Empire Theatre, the ENB has a second home in the city.

And after the '07 World Premiere of The Snow Queen in Liverpool – the dancers and orchestra return with the company's spectacular production of The Sleeping Beauty.

Expect grand classical choreography that reawakens the magic of the world's favourite fairy tale in an enchanted world of castles and curses, forests and fairies.

ballet.org.uk

Throughout '08

The Potting Shed

Fitzcarraldo, Canning Dock

A Liverpool Commission

Commissioned by Liverpool Culture Company for '08

Walk the Plank's theatre ship - the Fitzcarraldo - presents on board monthly cabaret evenings throughout '08.

Guest 'Head Gardeners' will choose the theme and curate the evening's entertainment, so that you can expect the best in organic ideas and a pest-free environment.

An exciting mix of the best of home-grown talent and special guests from across Europe present comedy, burlesque, magic, impro, theatre and spoken word, with installations, assignations, and music aplenty.

The house band will entertain with tunes to suit each evening's theme as guest singers, and late night DJs offer unusual tunes from Balkan beats to deviant country.

 In turn you're expected to dress up, turn up, and be up for something a bit different.

Parking at the Albert Dock. Entrance off the Strand.

walktheplank.co.uk

"In Liverpool it seemed that almost every Scouser alive was involved in some way in the bid. It is a solid base to build out from and to welcome into."
Miranda Sawyer, '08 Judge

LIVERPOOL ECHO

WE DID IT!
Liverpool: European Capital of Culture 2008

A year to Participate

Participation in all its forms is central to '08.

From a major platform for people to express their talents via 'open culture', to an in-depth 'creative communities' programme, Liverpool's European Capital of Culture is unique both in depth, quality and engagement.

Liverpool has a long and laudable history of work involving communities; organisations across the city have developed cutting-edge community art work that has influenced the world.

In June '03, when Liverpool won the '08 bid, there was recognition of this incredible history and the place it could have in the city's future.

The creative communities programme has forged partnerships across sectors such as health, environment and sport connecting culture to the regeneration of the city. It has involved over 100,000 people, 3,000 plus artists and hundreds of arts organisations.

The people of Liverpool are integral to the '08 programme, as they were in the bid, and as every page of this book demonstrates.

In this section are some specific examples of how Liverpool is engaging its people and using '08 to showcase their creativity.

8 highlights in

OPEN CULTURE

Open Culture is a collaborative project aiming to ensure widespread mass participation in '08.

Through verse, publication, and physical artefact the year will provide touchstones for future generations to build and reflect upon Liverpool's cultural life.

It is led by Prof Phil Redmond and supported by Liverpool Culture Company with three goals:

· to open a cultural conversation with, by and about the people of Liverpool and its region to explore who, what and where they come from

· to open up new avenues through which new talent can be encouraged and a cultural legacy beyond '08

· to open access to existing institutions by encouraging them to find innovative ways to reach new audiences

Open Culture projects include:

· 800 Lines for 800 Years - collated by BBC Radio Merseyside. A saga about the city's history written by public submission, moderated by Roger McGough

· Capital of Cultural Bench - an open design competition run through the Liverpool ECHO

· Liverpool Song - orchestrated by Radio City, this project aims to draw on Liverpool's musical heritage and find a new "song for Liverpool" post '08

· Scouse Map - The Daily Post asks the people of Liverpool to redefine their city boundaries from a cultural perspective

· Open Culture Portal - an online portal at the International Centre for Digital Content (ICDC) will collate and disseminate the project's activities, as well as provide an exhibition space and cultural forum

The Open Culture portal will be available to other cultural institutions to use to promote and support their own initiatives, as well as the ones outlined above.

open.culture.org.uk

In Parks:

Throughout '08
Fragrant
at the Bluecoat

Liverpool's Botanical Collection, now partly housed in Croxteth Country Park, inspires a series of free activities and performances (see page 054).

At the Bluecoat you will be able to:

· walk among giant 'plant life' in our garden and have fun making your own plant costume

· learn about William Roscoe and the Botanical Collection through a shadow puppet show and join in with your own puppet made with advice from our team

· try your hand at botanical drawing and create your own imaginative descriptions of the plants you have drawn, working with a poet and an artist

Fragrant will take place during school holidays and at weekends and some activities may be pre-booked.

In addition, a group of adults with learning disabilities from L8 and Fazakerley Resource Centres will create a series of murals featuring plants from the collection.

Another group will work with a costume maker and live artist to create amazing costumes, to perform in the garden at the Bluecoat and in the Lord Mayor's Parade (see page 069).

thebluecoat.org.uk

June
Alice in Wonderland
Presented by Spike Theatre

Liverpool 14 - 15; Knowsley 21- 22; Halton 28 - 29

Performed by a cast of 40 utilising puppetry, live music, and song, some of Merseyside's lesser-known parks are transformed into a magical wonderland. In its fifth year, Theatre in the Park, adds an extra park in the borough of Halton in '08. A book of how to stage your own outdoor theatre events is being written.

Supported by Liverpool Culture Company, Arts Council England and Knowsley MBC.

In Schools:

Over the last five years every school in Liverpool has been working on projects supporting the Liverpool '08 themed years programme.

Throughout '08, Liverpool schools present:

The Orrery

This dramatic mechanical sculpture symbolises Liverpool as 'the centre of the creative universe'. The giant structure explores and celebrates cultural organisations and the '08 highlights in the form of planets, suns, moons and stars creating a Liverpool '08 solar system. The project visits primary schools throughout '08 and showcase at events throughout the year. There is a wealth of performances, exhibitions and participatory events, which young people can engage in. This project will excite, inspire and engage young people in art forms they are familiar with, those they are not and combinations beyond their imaginations!

Generation 21

Children and young people will become city planners as they create designs for a healthy, 21st century city. Taking as its stimulus the innovations of Leonardo Da Vinci; his blueprints for flight, inventions and the human body, and the forward thinking of Le Corbusier (see page 160). Generation 21 - schools will collaborate with creative practitioners to produce 21 new commissions. The commissions will explore the theme of 'Generation 21'; innovation, built environment, health and well-being. This groundbreaking work will form the centrepiece for the Creative Learning Networks Conference; a national education conference on the 16 October at the new ECHO Arena.

Tales...
from far away and the house next door

Over 20 different further and higher education establishments come together in a glorious story from here and far away. The collaborative work will culminate into a site-specific extravaganza - Arabian Nights in theory, Scouse in essence - in a final performance at St George's Hall in September.

The project will be developed and delivered by Toxteth TV.

Little Acorns

The little people's programme for '08. Buildings dens, magical journeys, stormy seas and blazing suns, singing songs, dressing up, acting out, taking part, making, shaking and playing and much, much more. The under-fives are joined by arts organisations - Fuse, Aspire, Wild About Words and Royal Liverpool Philharmonic Orchestra.

Developed by Liverpool Culture Company, Liverpool Children's Services Early Years Team and Early Arts Forum.

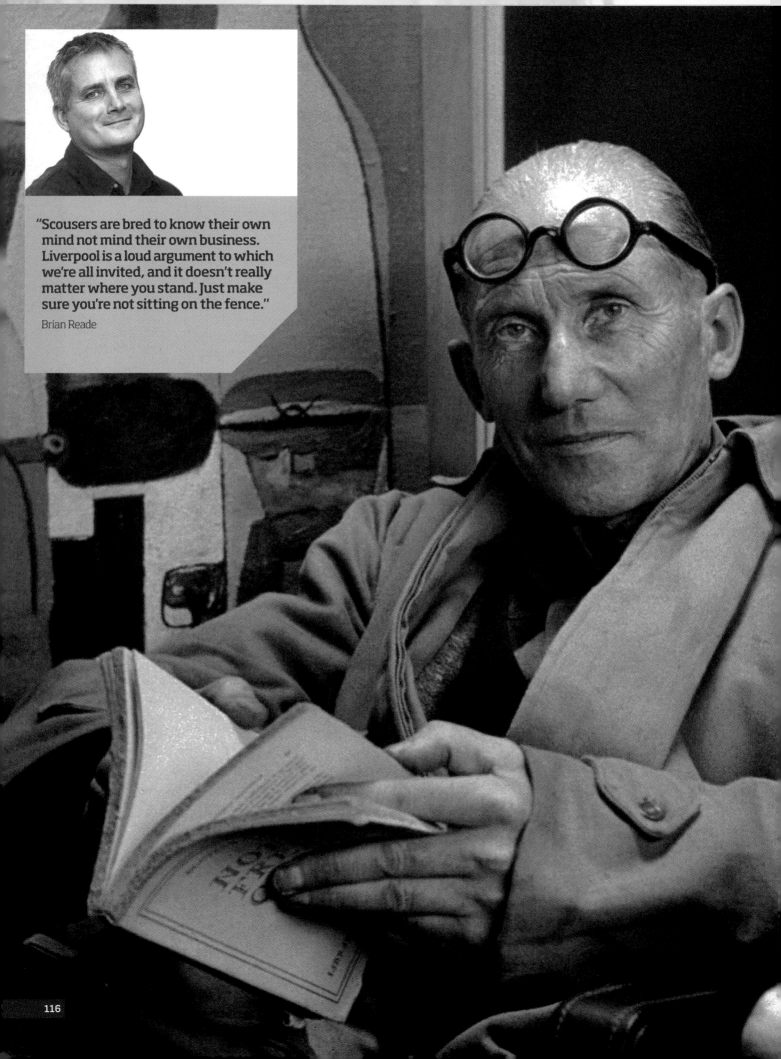

"Scousers are bred to know their own mind not mind their own business. Liverpool is a loud argument to which we're all invited, and it doesn't really matter where you stand. Just make sure you're not sitting on the fence."

Brian Reade

A year of
Conversation

Liverpool is a city of philosophers and poets, cutting-edge contemporary visual art and an ambitious new buildings programme that is changing not only the landscape of its core and heritage buildings, but also the way people relate to this physical renaissance.

In '08 the scene is set for enlightened cultural exchange, light-hearted banter and an intellectual legacy that will benefit future generations.

The major exhibition celebrating the life and work of architect Le Corbusier (left) is the starting point for a symposium attracting some of the leading figures in architecture to debate and discuss our built environment.

At the other end of this diverse strand, Ken Dodd presents his thoughts of Liverpool's unique contribution to comedy.

BBC Radio 3 and BBC Radio Merseyside's Free Thinking Festival of ideas explores FACT's theme of Human Futures, shifting boundaries and ideas around body, mind, and world.

This year of conversation also embraces the city's long-standing lecture series – the Roscoe Lectures plus a wide range of arts conferences, seminars and workshops.

The last word may be with the voice of the future as The European Youth Parliament and The Big Hope are two key events where the young of Europe and beyond address global issues.

8 highlights in

To July

The Infinite Sea of Possibilities

Arts in Regeneration (AiR)

This programme delivers creative learning experiences for people with mental health distress and for learners with special needs/ learning disabilities.

Accredited workshops in creative writing, drama, visual arts, film, animation, ICT and digital media produce high quality products for advocacy, skills development, and fun and for sale.

In partnership with Liverpool City Council Adult Learning Services, PSS and other service providers city-wide.

artsinregeneration.co.uk

January - December

Literate Medicine

Liverpool Medical Institution, Mount Pleasant

It is said that medical students and doctors should read more widely to improve communication with their patients.

Here a varied programme of lectures from people such as author Germaine Greer (6 December) and former BBC arts correspondent Rosie Millard (14 February) and literate doctors such as Raymond Tallis (13 March) say what books they think their doctors should be reading.

Liverpool Medical Institution is one of the oldest medical societies in the world. Admission to events requires membership, but some will be open by registering on-line.

lmi.org.uk

January - November

Roscoe Lecture Series '08

All lectures at St George's Hall, Lime Street (see listings below)

Through the Foundation for Citizenship, Liverpool John Moores University presents the city's most exciting and challenging public lecture series.

This year the people of Liverpool once again have an opportunity to listen to, and to question some of the most highly respected local and national public figures.

14 January, 5.00pm
Trude Levi and **Philomene Uwamaliya**
'Holocaust Survivors'

24 January, 5.00pm
Clive Tyldesley, Sports Commentator, ITV Sports
'Liverpool - City of Sport'

18 February, 12.30pm
Stephen Broadbent, Sculptor
'Liverpool - City of Sculpture'

19 March, 5.00pm
Professor **Ian Tracey,** Organist and Master of Choristers of Liverpool Cathedral
'Liverpool - City of Music'

29 April, 5.00pm
Lord Heseltine
'Liverpool - Reflections and Changes'

15 May, 5.00pm
George Davies
'Liverpool - City of Fashion'

9 June, 5.00pm
Rt Rev Dr John Sentamu, Archbishop of York
'Liverpool - Where Religious Faith is Part of the Solution, Not the Problem'

19 June, 5.00pm
Peter Sissons, Broadcaster
'Liverpool - City of Media'

18 September, 5.00pm
Professor the **Lord Rees of Ludlow**
'Liverpool - City that Looks Beyond Itself'

6 October, 5.00pm
Loyd Grossman, Chairman, National Museums Liverpool
'Liverpool - City of Arts and Culture'

3 November, 12.30pm
Dr Brian Jacques, Author
'Liverpool - City of Literature'

4 December, 5.00pm
Roger McGough, Performance Poet
'In Conversation With...'

ljmu.ac.uk/citizen

30 January - 2 February
British Dance Edition
Debates and Talks
Venue tbc

British Dance Edition (BDE) is one of the foremost events in the UK dance calendar (see page 089).

Taking place in Liverpool for the first time BDE will run a number of debates and sessions, to complement its eclectic and diverse contemporary dance programme.

BDE is a festival, a marketplace, a gathering and a celebration. This prestigious showcase will attract hundreds of national and international dance promoters to Liverpool, in search of the latest talent and ideas in British dance.

bde2008.co.uk

11 March, 5.30 - 7.30pm
Circelation
unitytheatre

Circelation's first public conversation in Liverpool will be an exploration of the territory covered by aerial dance and look at examples of British and international practice, with a focus on artists, choreographers and creative riggers.

A panel of leading voices will lead the discussion to which eminent voices from the dance and aerial performance sectors will be invited alongside journalists/writers and audiences.

The conversation will look to develop a deeper understanding about the roots of 'aerial dance', and to discuss it alongside contemporary dance, as a sports/outdoor pursuits activity and the more obvious association with aerial circus.

In association with Merseyside Dance Initiative.

10 - 15 March 'Harnessing Performance' workshop.

merseysidedance.co.uk
circelation.co.uk

19 March
'08 Carnival Olympiad Seminar
Cornerstone Building, Haigh Street

The UK's carnival arts sector explores the opportunities over the next four years and beyond.

The aim is to identify development needs and to create an action plan to ensure a cohesive approach to maximising participation.

Participation in the seminar will be open to anyone involved with the sector, with representation from professional carnival arts companies, creative programmers, Arts Council England (ACE) officers, and from local authority officers playing a key facilitation role in enabling carnival activity.

The seminar is being coordinated on behalf of ACE by ArtReach.

carnivalseminar08.org.uk
artscouncil.org.uk

Throughout '08
The Contact Sessions
Contacting the World

Various venues

In the months leading up to Liverpool hosting Contacting the World in July '08 (see page 096), Contact will be co-ordinating a series of sessions in collaboration with Hope Street Ltd and 20 Stories High, exploring the world of theatre created by young people.

These sessions will be a unique opportunity to share ideas about the role of young people in creating new theatre work, supporting artistic excellence and emerging artists and developing an intercultural and international approach to making theatre.

contact-theatre.org

1 - 2 April

Ken Dodd and Liverpool's Laughter Makers

St George's Concert Room, William Brown Street

One of the most defining cultural characteristics of Liverpool is its humour.

And the legendary Ken Dodd's gift to '08 is a very special celebration of the great comedians from the city's past.

According to this master mirth-maker, their light-hearted approach to life proved to be one of the country's most effective weapons against Hitler.

In a unique lecture, Dodd talks about the life and impact of comedians from Music Hall Star Billy Matchett via ITMA Radio legend Tommy Handley, and great characters like Ted Ray, Rob Wilton, Beryl Orde and Avril Angers who Victoria Wood adored working with.

In the words of Arthur Askey "Ay thang yew!"

liverpool08.com

28 April

The Business Convention

Arena and Convention Centre Liverpool, Kings Dock

This is the ultimate gathering of business, government and skills leaders, with talks on how they applied a creative entrepreneurial approach to grow their businesses into global companies.

The event also provides an understanding of future market trends from the most successful budding entrepreneurs and how to support Britain's next generation of leaders.

Keynote speakers include:
· Sir Terry Leahy, Chief Executive, Tesco plc
· Digby, Lord Jones of Birmingham, KT, Minister of State for Trade and Investment
· David Frost, Director General, British Chambers of Commerce

Hosted by the British Chambers of Commerce
thebusinessconvention.com

3 - 5 May

Happy 20th Birthday Tate Liverpool

Albert Dock

A special weekend of events will mark 20 years of Tate Liverpool.

The public are invited to build a den in the Ground Floor Gallery, follow the Light Procession through the city or leave a wish for the future on the dock.

Some well known faces will lead tours around the exhibitions and watch out for special treats prepared by artists.

There's also a Late at Tate Birthday Special with music, dancing, film screenings, food and drink.

tate.org.uk/liverpool

May

Physical Fest 4

Presented by Momentum and Hope Street Ltd

Various venues

The UK's annual physical theatre workshop and performance festival will explore and celebrate acrobatics, Butoh, Grotowski, Suzuki and physical theatre from national and international practitioners.

There's also a jam performance, evening classes, a site-specific performance from participants and two international performances.

It aims to introduce powerful and experimental movement forms and styles, to bring international work to Liverpool, to research into body expression, exchange information as well as finding different ways in producing theatre material.

momentumtheatre.com
hope-street.org

20 - 22 June

Liverpool Open Source City

Presented by SoundNetwork and folly

WORLD PREMIERE

Commissioned by Liverpool Culture Company for '08

Liverpool is infamous for its innovative uses of electricity.

From the birth of the power grid (Sebastian Ferranti) to the early computer game industry (Psygnosis/Ocean Software/ZTT) to musicians like Julian Cope and all the way back to The Beatles.

This informal summit of innovative workshops, talks, and gigs builds on that legacy. Presented by artists, collectives and programmers working with open source software in sound, music and media art; join us to explore the debate on resources, creativity and property in the digital age.

You could be a computer expert or a technophobe, a new guitar band, an Apple Mac obsessive, a hip hop producer, a cubase user with no money, a digital artist, a youth worker, a singer songwriter, a teacher, a writer or just someone who wants to know more. Learn how to do creative things with electricity for free!

soundnetwork.org.uk
folly.co.uk

4 - 11 June

The Big Hope

**Hope University, Hope Park Campus
and various venues**

To mark the European Parliament's Year of Intercultural Dialogue, Liverpool Hope University brings together 1,000 young people (18-35 years) from across the world who have faith and are potential leaders of their communities.

They will consider urgent issues such as 'The Dignity of Human Life', 'Conflict Resolution' and 'Europe's Contribution to a More Humane Global Society' and look to create books, performances and DVDs.

Keynote speakers include: Rt Rev Dr John Sentamu, Archbishop of York; Pius Ncube, Archbishop of Buluwayo; Cherie Booth, QC; Stephen Green, Chairman of HSBC; Sushobva Barve of Delhi and many others.

Other aspects include 24/7 prayer, a social and cultural programme and an online community which will precede and follow The Big Hope.

The Big Hope will end at Liverpool Cathedral with the Liverpool 2008 International Faith Declaration, led by Lord David Alton.

It will reconvene in Liverpool in 2018 to assess progress.

hope.ac.uk/thebighope

creativity

poetic

vivid

12 - 14 June

Magical Mysterious Regeneration Tour:
Artists, Architecture and the Future of the City

What are the methods and meanings of urban regeneration?

Here Liverpool provides a live platform for an international conference, debating themes such as: 'Artists' Collectives and City Culture', 'Architects, Planning and the Politics of Regeneration', and 'City Life: Poverty and Power around the World'.

Historians and critics, artists and architects, administrators and curators will take artist-led bus tours and regeneration tours and will provide forums for critical debate on the purposes, benefits and costs of regeneration.

Finally, the conference will feature a research students' mini-conference, at which nine postgraduate students will give papers on regeneration topics.

Organised by Tate Liverpool and the University of Liverpool's Centre for Architecture and the Visual Arts (CAVA)

liv.ac.uk
tate.org.uk/liverpool

17 - 24 July

European Youth Parliament

St George's Hall, Lime Street

Nearly 300 young people from 30 countries will gather for a 10-day session of the European Youth Parliament to share ideas, culture and experience.

The sitting will culminate in the announcement of 15 resolutions which will be sent to the European Parliament.

Event organiser is Michael Leyland, Vice-President of European Youth Parliament United Kingdom (EYPUK).

Board of trustees include: Rt. Hon David Milliband, Secretary of State for Foreign & Commonwealth Affairs; Rt. Hon Peter Mandelson, Member of the European Commission; Councillor Warren Bradley, Leader of Liverpool City Council and Deputy Chair of the Liverpool Culture Company; George Howarth, MP for Knowsley North & Sefton East and Chair of the '08 All Party Parliamentary Group.

Supported by Liverpool Culture Company

liverpool08.com

25 - 27 July

YPPT International Conference

The Cornerstone, Haigh Street

The platform event for the Young People's Participatory Theatre (YPPT) project will share ideas, practice and debate issues of significance for the worldwide YPPT sector.

Led by young people it will celebrate, play and explore new ideas and approaches as well as sharing the results of the YPPT programme to date.

The YPPT programme team and organisers of 'Contacting the World' (a biennial international theatre project) are working together to enhance the experience of others taking part in the '08 programme.

The aim is to support a more entrepreneurial and innovative culture where young artists and practitioners collaborate across the performing arts, connecting with the wider creative industries here in the UK and abroad.

artscouncil.org.uk

6 - 11 September

The British Association's Festival of Science

University of Liverpool

One of Europe's largest and longest established festivals of its kind.

Typically the festival hosts over 250 events, with more than 400 leading scientists and social commentators.

The festival programme provides a rich mix of talks, debates, exhibitions, hands-on activities and excursions in a broad variety of venues and locations across the host city and beyond.

liv.ac.uk/08/science
the-ba.net/the-ba

1 - 2 October
The Liverpool Summit

Arena and Convention Centre Liverpool, Kings Dock

The Liverpool Summit is about transforming the future.

It's about bold leadership, it's about changing attitudes, and it's about learning from and engaging with leading minds whose ideas and vision have already transformed the way we think about our world.

The two days will be packed full of radical lessons and groundbreaking ideas from 'gurus', corporate leaders and statesmen. Key speakers include:

· Clayton Christensen
· Charles Handy
· Will Hutton
· Sir Terry Leahy
· Renee Mauborgne
· Chris Patten
· Michael Porter

theliverpoolsummit.com

31 October - 2 November
Free Thinking Festival

Presented by BBC Radio 3 and Radio Merseyside

FACT, Wood Street and various venues

Debate, performance, talks, provocation, humour, surprise - this festival of ideas returns for a third year.

The major theme of '08 is Human Futures, part of the year-long programme in FACT (Foundation for Art and Creative Technology) exploring shifting boundaries and ideas around My Body, My Mind and My World.

Expect to hear leading thinkers from the arts, sciences, philosophy, politics and new technology, plus music and specially commissioned drama amidst lectures, debates and events inviting active audience participation.

There will be plenty of ways to get involved during the weekend and in advance online.

Free Thinking is recorded for broadcast and can be heard again online for seven days after broadcast.

bbc.co.uk/radio3/freethinking/2008

THE LIVERPOOL SUMMIT

Transforming the Future

Also in November: Cornerstone Festival p 030 and Sleeping Beauty p 104

25 - 27 November

Towards a
New Urbanism

An international symposium
on the 21st Century City

Organised by the **RIBA Trust** and **The Academy of Urbanism**
In association with 'Le Corbusier – The Art of Architecture' Exhibition,
and The Urbanism Awards.

**Symposium and Debate: Design Academy,
Liverpool John Moores University, Mount Pleasant**

Urbanism Awards Dinner: St George's Hall, Lime Street

**Exhibition: The Crypt, Metropolitan Cathedral
of Christ the King, Brownlow Hill (see page 160)**

Last Thursday of every month

Late at Tate Liverpool

Albert Dock

If you never seem to find the time to see art, or if you want somewhere new to meet up for a drink with friends then this is your chance.

The gallery will stay open until 9.00pm and you can expect poetry readings and themed talks in the gallery space, music in the foyer, and the shop and cafe will be open late too. One of the UK's best collections of modern and contemporary art.

tate.org.uk/liverpool

Also in December: The Rightful Owners of the Song p 031

"You have history, you have sport, you have culture - you have Olympians. ...This is a city that really does know how to connect culture (and) sport with communities."

Lord Sebastian Coe

A winning spirit

134

A year in Sport

Sport is integral to Liverpool's DNA.

It has infused a passion, in player and supporter, that defines the city to millions the world over.

From the world's first rugby club, Britain's first chess club and the invention of the goalnet, to the sporting cathedrals of Aintree, Anfield and Goodison, Liverpool has made an indelible mark on how we all spend our leisure time.

Today the city is a centre of excellence in boxing, football, gymnastics, swimming and tennis and has developed *Sportslinx* - Europe's leading youth fitness and talent identification programme.

Underpinning all this is a desire to play - and win - as was evident in the bid for European Capital of Culture status.

In '08 expect to see sport playing its role to the full as new venues open, such as a 50m pool at Wavertree and the ECHO Arena Liverpool, which can stage all major indoor sports and hosts the BBC Sports Personality of the Year Awards on 14 December.

As well as following its football teams, get a ringside seat at the European Boxing Championships, catch The Open at Royal Birkdale, and encourage a new generation of stars in events like the English Schools Cross-country Championships.

Then there's international tennis, the finale of the Tour of Britain and the World Firefighters Games.

And in '08 history comes full circle for the city which inspired a global movement, by staging Olympiads in the 1860s, as Liverpool begins the Cultural Olympiad for London 2012.

8 highlights in

25 - 26 January
Supercross

ECHO Arena Liverpool, Kings Dock

One of the world's most spectacular sporting events Supercross is the indoor version of motocross.

For this high-octane event the Arena will be transformed into a four-lane dirt obstacle course using more than 5,000 tons of soil.

High aerial jumps and challenging course obstacles will be created for some of the world's top riders.

This event is non-stop, edge-of-your-seat excitement featuring awe-inspiring action.

accliverpool.com

8 March
English Schools Cross-country Championships

Sefton Park, Croxteth Drive

Around 2,000 young athletes aim to follow in the footsteps of Steve Cram, Steve Ovett, Paula Radcliffe and Kelly Holmes by seeking glory at Britain's biggest cross-country running event.

It is the first time the Championships have been held in Liverpool since 1994.

A huge turnout of spectators is expected for this amazing, free sporting spectacle.

liverpool08.com

20 March
'08 Premier Darts

ECHO Arena Liverpool, Kings Dock

The '08 Premier League Darts features the best eight players in the sport battling over three months in one of the game's most exciting tournaments.

Phil 'The Power' Taylor has been the Premier League champion for the past three years but current Ladbrokes.com World Darts Champion Raymond van Barneveld is aiming to topple him.

See if he succeeds once more as the tournament is played on 14 successive Thursday nights around the UK from 31 January.

The top four progress to the play-offs at the end of May – with every dart screened live on Sky Sports.

"Liverpool is one of the world's great sporting cities and we can't wait to give darts fans there the chance to see the very best players in the sport."

PDC Chairman Barry Hearn

planetdarts.tv
accliverpool.com

13 - 16 March
International Table Tennis Tournament
(Pre-Paralympic qualifier)

Greenbank Sports Academy, Greenbank Lane

Watch high quality competition amongst top disabled players as they set their sights on qualification for the Beijing Paralympics.

ipttc.org

Throughout '08
Disability Sports Festival

Various venues

A range of sports taster sessions aimed at promoting increased sports participation amongst disabled people, their families and their carers.

Primarily focussed on the Greenbank Sports Academy, the festival offers a variety of taster sessions. No past experience required.

greenbanksportsacademy.co.uk

Also in March: Liverpool Reads p 036 and LEAP Festival p 091

ANTHEMIC

The pulse
the beat

jazz

3 - 5 April
Grand National
Aintree Racecourse, Ormskirk Road

ANNUAL EVENT

One of the highlights of the sporting year, The Grand National captures the imagination of millions.

It consistently produces thrilling finishes and heart-warming stories as horse and rider try to conquer the mighty Aintree fences.

Liverpool's flair for style has become an increasingly popular side-show with Ladies Day now a major fixture in the national fashion calendar.

A global television event, Aintree has made huge improvements to stadia in recent years and in '07 an indoor, equestrian centre opened to give the course an all-year-round sporting calendar.

aintree.co.uk
thejockeyclub.co.uk

Also in April: Twilight City p 018 and Around the City in Eighty Pubs p 155

6 - 12 May

British Open Squash Championships

Liverpool Cricket Club, Aigburth Drive and ECHO Arena Liverpool, Kings Dock

Liverpool will stage the UK's most prestigious squash event as the world's top players fight it out to become the Dunlop British Open Champion.

Liverpool Cricket Club will host the preliminary rounds with the finals (10 - 12 May) being hosted on the glass court at the ECHO Arena Liverpool.

squashsite.org.uk/bo/2008
accliverpool.com

24 - 25 May

Liverpool International Handball Festival

Greenbank Sports Academy, Greenbank Lane and Liverpool John Moores University (I.M Marsh Campus)

A celebration of handball set with a multi-cultural event that includes a wide age range of participants, male and female and which is inclusive of disability sport.

liverpool.handballclub.co.uk

24 - 25 May

European Speedminton Championships '08

Liverpool Tennis Centre, Wellington Road

These first championships will feature over 100 athletes from 14 European nations competing in the world's fastest growing racquet sport.

liverpool.handballclub.co.uk

31 May

National Junior Open Karate Tournament

Greenbank Sports Academy, Greenbank Lane

Liverpool has always been a hotbed for martial arts, and the city has a history of producing national, European, Commonwealth and indeed world Karate champions.

This fantastic event will see the very best exponents of this ancient discipline take part in a national junior open event.

liverpool08.com

Also in May: Southport Jazz Festival p 020 and Metal Pavilion at Edge Hill Station p 046

21 - 22 June

Gymnastics International
Featuring GB, Romania and Italy

Liverpool Gymnastics Centre of Excellence, Park Road

Leading female gymnasts compete in this tri-nations warm-up event for the Beijing Olympic Games.

The GB team will feature Liverpool gymnast and World Champion on bars Beth Tweddle.

Romania, previous Olympic Team Champions, are in Liverpool for only their third time.

liverpool.gov.uk
british-gymnastics.org

10 - 15 June

Liverpool International Tennis

Calderstones Park, Menlove Avenue

ANNUAL EVENT

One of tennis' success stories of the decade is the rise and rise of the Liverpool International.

Based in a public park, where John Lennon played as a child, the competition has hosted many top ranked players and Grand Slam winners including Marat Safin, who won the inaugural title in '02.

Its legends event has been graced by players such as Bjorn Borg and Martina Navratilova. And attracting up-and-coming British players is also a strong feature, with Wimbledon mixed-doubles champion Jamie Murray a previous competitor.

The tournament's other main aim is supporting kids' tennis and some 5,000 youngsters receive coaching every year with elite players getting classes from the stars.

liverpooltennis.co.uk

4 July

Clipper Round-the-World Yacht Race

Mersey Waterfront

The return of the Clipper '07 - '08 Round-the-World Yacht Race is a maritime spectacle befitting a great river. As the world's fastest, non-professional, yachting race finishes at the entrance to the Mersey, a flotilla of boats will follow the international yachts up the river to a hero's welcome for all. After 35,000 miles and 12 months of intense ocean racing expect jubilant scenes.

clipperroundtheworld.com

5 July

Merseyside Youth Games

Wavertree Sports Complex, Wellington Road

ANNUAL EVENT

The largest youth sport event in the region offers year-round sporting opportunities to over 60,000 children. By competition weekend, 3,500 children will compete to be Merseyside's finest. Now in its 14th year, the partnership that delivers the Games has generated a significant amount of investment to develop a vibrant sporting infrastructure of clubs, coaches and volunteers across the region.

merseysidesport.com

Also in July: Everyword p 038 and Movieplex p 061

22 - 25 July

4-Nations Junior Chess Championships

Liverpool John Moores University
(I.M Marsh Campus)

The national junior teams of the home nations compete for the Glorney Cup (boys) and the Faber Cup (girls). These two trophies are the oldest in the world for junior players. The Glorney Cup celebrates its 60th anniversary, and the Faber Cup its 40th, during '08.

liverpoolchessfoundation.co.uk

27 July - 9 August

British Chess Championships

St George's Hall, Lime Street

The world's oldest chess championships, running since 1866, are in Liverpool for the very first time. Over 2,000 players - from grandmasters to amateurs - will contest to be the overall British Champion. Further tournaments decide the champions in age groups from under-9 through to senior citizen. Games are broadcast 'live' on the internet.

bcf.org.uk
liverpoolchessfoundation.co.uk

29 July - 3 August

The Liverpool-Knowsley International Youth Soccer Festival

Mather Avenue playing fields, Allerton

ANNUAL EVENT

This FIFA approved tournament provides local leading boys and girls teams a chance to participate against international opposition and experiencing other cultures through the international language of sport.

The '07 event attracted over 100 teams including 22 international sides. Off the field there is a hectic social schedule as teams get to visit the top attractions across the city and North West.

Staged in picturesque university playing fields in south Liverpool, this annual event is one of Europe's premier youth soccer tournaments.

lksoccertournament.com

Also in August: Creamfields p 023 and Community Shakespeare p 039

1 August
Liverpool Community Games
Wavertree Sports Complex, Wellington Road

ANNUAL EVENT

The Liverpool Community Games will see groups from across the city's five neighbourhoods come together for a mass participatory sports festival.

The event will promote friendly rivalry with a balance between competition and taster activities.

liverpool08.com

13 August
Merseyside Community Youth Games
Wavertree Sports Complex, Wellington Road

ANNUAL EVENT

This event at Wavertree Sports Complex will bring together athletes from across Merseyside and Halton to participate and compete in a range of sports competition and taster activities.

Delivered by Merseyside Sport, the event will showcase grass-roots sports participation across the county.

A Liverpool representative team will emerge to take part in the Merseyside Community Youth Games later in the year.

merseysidesport.com/events

16 - 17 August
National Table Tennis Grand Prix
Liverpool Tennis Centre, Wellington Road

The cream of Britain's table tennis players gather to compete in one of four 'majors' on the national governing body calendar.

The tournament is part of a growing partnership between Liverpool City Council's sports development and events section, The English Table Tennis Association and the local table tennis fraternity.

englishtabletennis.org.uk

"Maritime commerce brought Liverpool not just wealth and employment, but also an air of cosmopolitanism that few cities in the world could rival, and it still has that sense about it. In Liverpool you still feel that you are in some place."

Bill Bryson

A year of Exploring

In Liverpool '08, the city's heritage reveals itself in many ways, internationally via Cities on the Edge, nationally through projects like Portrait of a Nation and locally in Around the City in Eighty pubs.

It emerges in the regeneration of its World Heritage waterfront, through the way in which it has built its music scene and its artistic community.

It is also manifest in its buildings, like the Bluecoat and Liverpool's magnificent St George's Hall - a neo-classical icon of the city's maritime wealth.

The city's modern day resurgence now emerges in its contemporary architecture from John Moores University's Art and Design Academy, the landmark waterfront Arena, Liverpool One and beyond that to 2010 and the opening of the Museum of Liverpool.

In '08, a programme exploring this heritage, and the people who helped forge this environment, will take you through 800 years of history and into the 21st century.

8 highlights in 08

5 January - 7 February

The Anne Frank Festival

Liverpool Cathedral, St James Mount

Alongside the commemoration of Holocaust Memorial Day, the centrepiece of this festival will be the presentation of the Anne Frank + You exhibition.

At the heart of this multi-media touring exhibition is the spirit of Anne Frank: her words, wisdom and values.

Inside Britain's biggest cathedral, explore the history of the Holocaust and compelling contemporary issues including racism in football, the right to wear religious symbols, bullying and the plight of child soldiers.

Using interviews with British teenagers, it presents questions about how we deal with conflict and how we contribute to society.

The festival will also include art and journalistic competitions for young people and musical performances.

Developed by the Anne Frank Trust UK, the Anne Frank House in Amsterdam and Oscar-winning film director John Blair.

annefrank.org

27 January

National Holocaust Memorial Day

Philharmonic Hall, Hope Street

The anniversary of the liberation of the Auschwitz-Birkenau concentration camp is designated as International Holocaust Memorial Day (HMD) by the UN. Liverpool will host the UK's national commemoration in '08.

NMD commemorates victims of the Holocaust as a result of Nazi persecution and in more recent genocides. It educates about the Holocaust, its lessons for the present day and prompts action, highlighting the dangers of racism, anti-semitism and all forms of discrimination.

hmd.org.uk

To Autumn

Merchant Palaces

Sudley House, Mossley Hill

The photographs in this exhibition were taken between 1888 and 1916, by the London-based firm Bedford Lemere and Co. One of the best architectural photographers of his day, Lemere travelled the country taking pictures of the homes of the rich and the wealthy of the late Victorian and Edwardian era. This work often brought Lemere to Liverpool, which was at the height of its prosperity as the second port of the British Empire.

liverpoolmuseums.org.uk/sudley

Also in March: European Union Youth Orchestra p 018 and Re-opening of the Bluecoat p 50

14 March

Globalization – the Making of Our World
The Royal Society of Antiquarians

St George's Concert Room, William Brown Street

Sir Neil Cossons traces the origins of today's world, the roots of globalization and its contemporary consequences, freedoms gained and distinctiveness lost, the death of distance, commodification and the cult of recency. The talk is part of the society's tercentenary festival.

sal.org.uk

7 April - 30 November

Liverpool's People and Places:
The Photography of E. Chambré Hardman

Various venues

Presented by The National Trust (NT)

This travelling exhibition aims to bring the photography of Edward Chambré Hardman to a wider audience. Hardman, who lived at 59 Rodney Street (now owned by the NT) between 1947-88, captured many scenes now changed forever, as well as Liverpool's inhabitants. The exhibition includes work by young people from Liverpool, who used Hardman's images to explore their own cultural heritage and background.

nationaltrust.org.uk

April - September

Around the City in Eighty Pubs

City wide

This will be a unique celebration of Liverpool's pubs and pub culture climaxing in a two-week festival of music, games, architecture, food and of course beer!

liverpool08.com

April - September

Out of the Shadows

St George's Heritage Centre, St John's Lane

A major project based around recorded reminiscences of older people with a range of physical and mental disabilities. The project will trace their stories from childhood through to institutionalisation to, attitudes of what we might call, 'normal people'. It explores too their sexuality and relationships and their treatment by society today, culminating in a provocative exhibition at St George's Hall.

liverpool08.com

12 July - 1 November '09

The Beat Goes On

World Museum Liverpool, William Brown Street

Liverpool's unique place in popular culture is the inspiration behind this exhibition. It showcases Merseyside's vibrant music scenes, bands and fans that over the past 60 years have played a major part in the city's life. From the Cavern to Creamfields, from Billy Fury to The Zutons, the exhibition will pay tribute to our very own 'Capital of Pop'.

liverpoolmuseums.org.uk/wml

To 27 September '09

Magical History Tour

Merseyside Maritime Museum, Albert Dock

This major exhibition documents 800 years of Liverpool's history. Stories will be told through the lives of ordinary people, the famous and the infamous. The exhibition also looks forward to the Liverpool of the future, reflecting aspirations and ambitions for the city in the 21st century and beyond.

liverpoolmuseums.org.uk/maritime

Also in July: Hope Street Ltd Public Art Programme p 072 and British Chess Championships p 144

23 August

Slavery Remembrance Day

Otterspool, South Liverpool

A series of free events, including a multi-faith Act of Reflection, is held in Liverpool annually to remember the victims of the transatlantic slave trade.

The city has a new focal point for this day with the International Slavery Museum (ISM) at the Albert Dock.

A second phase of the project, due to open in 2010, will include the development of a new visitor-focused education centre with an events programme of performance, public lectures and debate using the newly-acquired Dock Traffic Office.

A research institute based in the museum is being developed in partnership with the University of Liverpool.

Liverpool Slavery Remembrance Initiative is a partnership between National Museums Liverpool, individuals from the city's black community, Liverpool City Council, Liverpool Culture Company and The Mersey Partnership.

liverpoolmuseums.org.uk/ism

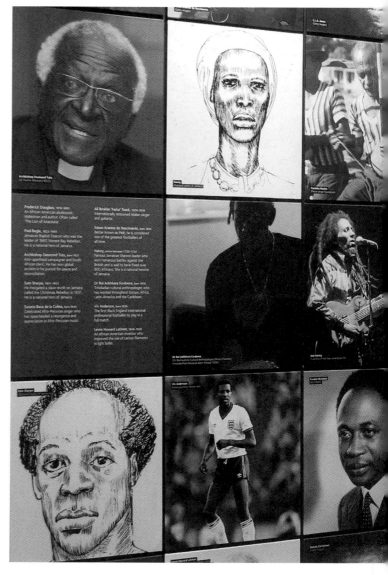

Download the free mp3 tour of Liverpool's Slave Trail at **liverpool08.com**

11 - 21 September

Heritage Open Days

Merseyside wide

From a weekend event a few years ago, hundreds of heritage buildings across Merseyside will open to the public -free of charge - for two weeks in '08.

There will be a supporting programme of community events including walks, tours and family activities.

**civictrust.org.uk
english-heritage.org.uk
liverpool08.com**

1 - 30 September

St George's Hall and I

St George's Hall, Lime Street

Liverpool's most important heritage building has a fond place in many a Liverpudlian's heart.

Over the last 150 years most people have a story to tell about St George's Hall be it concerts, court cases, vigils to cup parades.

This project culminating in an exhibition enables these memories to be shared.

liverpool08.com

Also in September: Phil Collins / Javier Tellez p 057 and Hope Street Festival p 077

2 October - 11 January '09

Le Corbusier - The Art of Architecture

The Crypt, Metropolitan Cathedral of Christ the King, Brownlow Hill

Liverpool stages the UK's biggest exhibition for 20 years on the 'greatest architect of the 20th century'- Le Corbusier.

Original architectural models, furniture, previously unpublished vintage prints, drawings, and paintings of the Swiss-born architect will all be housed in one of the UK's most dramatic spaces - the Crypt of the Metropolitan Cathedral, designed by Sir Edwin Luytens.

Le Corbusier: The Art of Architecture has been organised by the Royal Institute of British Architects (RIBA) Trust.

architecture.com
liverpool08.com

11 October

RIBA Stirling Prize

BT Convention Centre, Kings Dock

The RIBA Stirling Prize is being held in Liverpool to mark the city's year as the European Capital of Culture.

Recognised as the most prestigious award for contemporary British architecture, the prize is announced and broadcast live in a Channel 4 programme, presented by Kevin McCloud.

Also presented on the evening are a number of special prizes recognising the diversity of British architecture, including awards for sustainability, the best school and the most outstanding new house.

architecture.com

November - March '09

Liverpool - Threshold to the Corners of the World

Victoria Gallery and Museum, Brownlow Hill

The re-opening of University of Liverpool's new £8m Victoria Gallery and Museum is celebrated with a unique photography exhibition of Liverpool and its people.

A total of 40 original images by Liverpool photographer Edward Chambré Hardman capture the city at a time it was influencing the world with its industrial, wartime and maritime activities.

Hardman's home - 59 Rodney Street - also contains a small display of Hardman's images . Most of the 142,000 photographs he took during his lifetime are undergoing conservation work and archiving at Liverpool Records Office.

The Victoria Gallery and Museum opens in July. Highlights of the refurbishment include a glass passenger lift within the clock tower.

Exhibition organised by The National Trust and University of Liverpool.

nationaltrust.org.uk
liv.ac.uk

1 November

North West Family History Fair

St George's Hall, Lime Street

Family history research is one of the most popular growing pastimes, with numbers exploring their personal heritage growing every year. If you want to explore your family tree, put this fair - packed with experts and how to guides - in your calendar.

nwgfhs.org.uk
liverpool08.com

Also in November: eighth blackbird p 030 and Made in Liverpool p 062

December
Labyrinth of Light
St George's Hall, Lime Street

Walk through a beautiful labyrinth of 800 candles, shimmering within the vast darkness of St George's Hall, whilst a dramatic fugue is played on the world-famous Willis organ.

liverpool08.com

162

December
Portrait of a Nation
Liverpool and nationwide

Over two years, young people across the UK have been exploring their heritage and identity, defining how the past is central to a vibrant present and optimistic future.

A series of events in 17 British cities will showcase the young people's arts and heritage projects, revealing what is special to them about where they come from.

Their work will culminate in a spectacular festival at the end of '08 to close the year-long Liverpool European Capital of Culture celebrations.

Each city will be adopted by a Liverpool neighbourhood, as communities celebrate their own cultural identity alongside that of their hosts.

Co-ordinated by Liverpool Culture Company, 17 member cities of the Urban Cultural Network and the Heritage Lottery Fund.

liverpool08.com
hlf.org.uk

Cities on The Edge

Cities on The Edge (CoTE) is a unique partnership of six European cities: Liverpool, England; Bremen, Germany; Gdansk, Poland; Istanbul, Turkey; Marseilles, France; Naples, Italy.

At Liverpool's invitation, these five cities have come together to examine their roles as historic ports and their sense of themselves as city states, as islands within their nation.

To explore these edgy and creative characteristics, Liverpool is welcoming hundreds of European artists, professionals, and young people to share and exchange ideas and experiences throughout '08.

8 CoTE highlights in '08:

January - December
Football: Life or Death

A documentary style film following supporters in Naples, Liverpool, Marseilles, Istanbul, all famous for their unconditional dedication to the passion of football. A supporter from each city will go and live with supporters from one of the other cities. There they experience immersion in daily life in a community where they probably speak a different language, have different cultural traditions, different values and beliefs.

4 - 6 March
Serious Organised Crime conference, BT Convention Centre plus fringe events at FACT

These include a lecture by Roberto Saviano, Italian author of 'Gomorrah: Italy's other mafia'; UK Film Premiere of 'Biutiful Cauntri', a feature length documentary on the Mafia's impact on the environment; and a debate on organised crime.

March - December
Reberth

An anthology of short fiction examining the changing face of Europe's port cities. This project also provides a forum for intercultural dialogue between writers, translators, cultural theorists from CoTE cities. Reberth will result in a publication, short story day of live readings and a student writing and translation scheme.

April - December
Coming and Going

This project asks questions about migration and looks at the impact of migrants upon the cultural life of the CoTE cities. Project takes form of interrelated events, produced in November, involving photography, music, food and radio broadcasts. Fortnight-long project will culminate in an event where issues can be shared and debated by artists, experts and members of the public.

1 - 3 May
Intercultural Cities Conference, St George's Hall

A major European conference for 300 delegates drawing people from across CoTE cities and wider Europe. Tackling major questions - what it means to be intercultural and defining the intercultural city. This is an official UK event for the European Year for Intercultural Dialogue for '08.

Summer
Streetwaves

Up to 100 unsigned bands will compete in heats across CoTE, with the best bands performing at the '08 Mathew Street Music Festival (see page 023). Liverpool winners will perform a European tour.

October - November
Photography on the Edge

Six photographers will produce work in all six cities, overseen by the renowned urban landscapes photographer John Davies. Theme will be the changing face of port cities, with an emphasis on social and environmental issues.

19 - 21 November
International Port Cities Conference

This event covers a range of themes including tourism, culture, heritage, planning, architecture and developers with a European dimension provided by CoTE partners.

liverpool08.com

In Focus:

Liverpool is in England - but is not of this country. Situated on the River Mersey and facing west onto the Atlantic its inspirations and attitudes have been forged by its seafaring community, its merchants, sailors and immigrants. The city has at various times been described as the capital of Wales and Ireland and America's eastern most city. With long established African, Arabic, Chinese, Jewish, Catholic and Protestant communities Liverpool is a city that has learnt to tolerate and celebrate different cultures.

Istanbul is at the furthest Eastern point of Europe and lays claim to be one of the most diverse cities in the world - where East and West meet. Its role as the bridgehead between Islam and Christianity is clearly pivotal. Historically Byzantium and later Constantinople, Istanbul has been the capital city of the Roman, Byzantine, Latin and Ottoman Empires. Today it is Turkey's most populous city and its cultural and financial centre. Located on the Bosphorus Strait, it is a World Heritage City and non-EU European Capital of Culture 2010.

Marseilles is probably the city in Europe with the strongest and most productive links with North Africa. Located on the Mediterranean Sea, it is France's largest port and second largest city. From the 1950s onwards the city served as an entrance for over a million immigrants, many of whom came in 1962 from Algeria.

Naples has also experienced a strong Islamic influence. This is noticeable in the local dialect, patisserie, urban form, and in some architectural motifs, as well as through trade links with the Middle East and North Africa. Naples is the largest and most prosperous city in southern Italy, but it is estimated four million of its citizens emigrated at the turn of the 20th century.

Gdansk a former Hanseatic city, known historically by the German name Danzig, lies on the southern coast of the Baltic Sea. The city is situated at the mouth of the Motlawa River, giving it a pivotal role in Poland's sea trade. Its shipyard was the birthplace of the Solidarity trade union movement, which led to the end of communist party rule in 1989.

Bremen, situated in North West Germany was also a Hanseatic City state. Situated along the river Weser, which leads to the North Sea, it is the second most populous city in North Germany. Bremen is also the oldest city state in the world. Home to Germany's oldest university, it is also host to the world's oldest fairground festival.

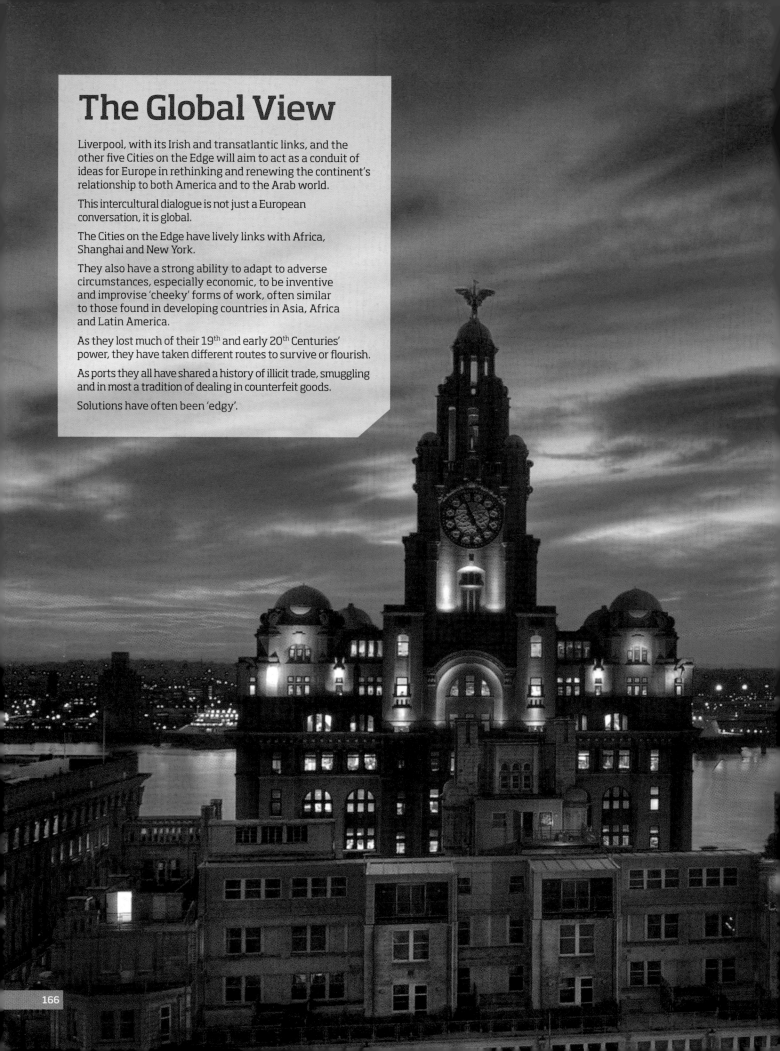

The Global View

Liverpool, with its Irish and transatlantic links, and the other five Cities on the Edge will aim to act as a conduit of ideas for Europe in rethinking and renewing the continent's relationship to both America and to the Arab world.

This intercultural dialogue is not just a European conversation, it is global.

The Cities on the Edge have lively links with Africa, Shanghai and New York.

They also have a strong ability to adapt to adverse circumstances, especially economic, to be inventive and improvise 'cheeky' forms of work, often similar to those found in developing countries in Asia, Africa and Latin America.

As they lost much of their 19th and early 20th Centuries' power, they have taken different routes to survive or flourish.

As ports they all have shared a history of illicit trade, smuggling and in most a tradition of dealing in counterfeit goods.

Solutions have often been 'edgy'.

'08 and Beyond

'08 is the European Year of Intercultural Dialogue.
Cities are the best setting for dialogue.

Cities on the Edge will celebrate, investigate and
compare experiences to discover what it means to be
an intercultural city, and what gives these six cities
their unique cultural identities.

A wide-ranging programme of thought-provoking
events will be used across opera, film, youth theatre
and literature to music, dance and gastronomy.

These projects will explore a variety of themes concerning
the six port cities, but which are of relevance to cities of
many different kinds across the globe.

These themes include :

· the rebelliousness of the six cities
· the 'hidden identities' of immigrants and outsiders
· football as a modern passion and even religion
· the cultural expressions of marginalised social groups
· the importance of the tangible and intangible heritage
  of ports in processes of urban regeneration
· the danger of urban standardisation
· interculturalism as a way to both combat prejudice and
  racism to encourage cultural, social and economic innovation.

The Liverpool team will work on these themes in
partnership with many different organisations, including
the European Opera Centre (see page 016), English Heritage,
the Royal Institute of British Architects, and local authorities
and cultural organisations in all six cities.

Exploring Our Museums and Galleries in '08:

National Museums Liverpool is England's only national museums group based entirely outside London. These unique venues (listed below) are home to fabulously varied collections covering everything from social history to space travel, entomology to ethnology, dinosaurs to docks, arts to archaeology. They're also open every day 10.00am-5.00pm. Free entry!

1 **World Museum Liverpool** combines historic treasures from across the globe with the latest interactive technology on everything from real live bugs to Egyptian mummies, prehistoric pottery to space exploration and Britain's only free Planetarium. William Brown Street, Liverpool city centre

2 **Walker Art Gallery** discover over six centuries of art at the national gallery of the north, home to one of Europe's finest collections of fine and decorative -from Renaissance masters to contemporary stars. William Brown Street, Liverpool city centre

3 **National Conservation Centre** is where science meets art. Conservators based here look after National Museums Liverpool's diverse collections. Everything from Roman sculpture to Cold War spacesuits comes here to be preserved and restored. Whitechapel, Liverpool city centre

4 **Lady Lever Art Gallery** displays British 18th and 19th century paintings, 18th century furniture and outstanding examples of Wedgwood and Chinese - all collected by William Hesketh Lever, the first Lord Leverhulme. Port Sunlight, Bebington, Wirral

5 **Sudley House** is home to the only Victorian merchant's art collection held in its original setting, with paintings by Gainsborough, Reynolds, Turner and Landseer bought by ship owner George Holt. Mossley Hill Road, Mossley Hill

6 **Merseyside Maritime Museum (MMM)** tells the history of Liverpool's central role as the gateway to the new world, how the Titanic, Lusitania and Empress of Ireland tragedies affected the city and how the port provided a lifeline in times of war and peace. Albert Dock, Liverpool city centre

7 **Customs and Excise Museum** reopens in May '08 as a brand new gallery in the basement of MMM. 'Seized: revenue and customs uncovered' will be the national museum of HM Revenue and Customs, drawing on contraband seizures and other archive material from all over the country. Albert Dock, Liverpool city centre

8 **International Slavery Museum** explores both the historical and contemporary aspects of slavery, addressing the many legacies of the slave trade and reveals many untold stories of bravery and rebellion amongst the enslaved people. Albert Dock, Liverpool city centre

One for the future:

Museum of Liverpool: opening in 2010, on Liverpool's World Heritage waterfront, the Museum of Liverpool will be a bigger and better version of the former museum, which had been a popular waterfront attraction since 1993. Go to **liverpoolmuseums.org.uk/mol** for news and updates.

Other museums and galleries:

For further information about Liverpool's wide range of independent museums and galleries please go to **artinliverpool.com** (see map on page 174).

FACT

Exploring '08 Calendar

Featured Events:

January

To 27 Sept '09:	**Magical History Tour**	liverpoolmuseums.org
To Autumn:	**Merchant Palaces**	liverpoolmuseums.org.uk
5-17:	**Treasures**	liverpool08.com
5-7 Feb:	**The Anne Frank Festival**	
		liverpoolcathedral.org.uk
27:	**National Holocaust Memorial Day**	
		liverpoolphil.com

March

14:	**Globalization - The Making of Our World**	
		sal.org.uk

April

To Sept:	**Around the City in Eighty Pubs**	liverpool08.com
To Sept:	**Out of the Shadows**	liverpool08.com
7-30 Nov:	**Liverpool's People and Places**	nationaltrust.org

May

1-3:	**Intercultural Cities Conference**	euclid.info

July

12-1 Nov '09:	**The Beat Goes On**	liverpoolmuseums.org.uk

August

	Barging-in	liverpool08.com
	tenantspin	liverpool08.com
23:	**Slavery Remembrance Day**	
		liverpoolmuseums.org.uk

September

11-21:	**Heritage Open Days**	civictrust.org.uk
1-30:	**St George's Hall and I**	liverpool08.com

October

2-11 Jan '09:	**Le Corbusier - The Art of Architecture**	
		architecture.com
11:	**RIBA Stirling Prize**	architecture.com

November

1:	**North West Family History Fair**	nwkfhs.org.uk
19-21:	**International Port Cities Conference**	
		liverpool08.com

December

	Labyrinth of Light	liverpool08.com
	Portrait of a Nation	liverpool08.com

 Download the free mp3 tour of Liverpool's World Heritage Trail at **liverpool08.com**

Exploring '08 Directory

Featured Venues:

Liverpool Cathedral
St James Mount L1 7AZ
0151 709 6271 liverpoolcathedral.org.uk

Merseyside Maritime Museum
Albert Dock L3 4AQ
0151 478 4499 liverpoolmuseums.org.uk/maritime

Metropolitan Cathedral of Christ The King
Hope Street L3 5TQ
0151 709 9222 liverpoolmetrocathedral.org

Philharmonic Hall
Hope Street L1 9BP
0151 210 2895 liverpoolphil.com

St George's Hall
Lime Street L1 1JH
0151 233 2008 liverpool08.com

Sudley House
Mossley Hill Road L18 5BX
0151 724 3245 liverpoolmuseums.org.uk/sudley

Victoria Gallery and Museum
Brownlow Hill L69 3GB
0151 794 200 liverpool.ac.uk

World Museum Liverpool
William Brown Street L3 8EN
0151 478 4393 liverpoolmuseums.org.uk/wml

Featured Organisations:

Anne Frank Trust	annfrank.org
Civic Trust	civictrust.org.uk
English Heritage	english-heritage.org.uk
EUCLID	euclid.info
European Opera Centre	operaeurope.org
FACT	fact.co.uk
Heritage Lottery Fund	hlf.org.uk
Liverpool Cathedral	liverpoolcathedral.org.uk
Liverpool City Council	liverpool.gov.uk
Metropolitan Cathedral	liverpoolmetrocathedral.org
National Museums Liverpool	liverpoolmuseums.org.uk
RIBA	architecture.com
Royal Liverpool Philharmonic Orchestra	liverpoolphil.com
Royal Society of Antiquaries	sal.org.uk
The Mersey Partnership	merseyside.org.uk
The National Trust	nationaltrust.org
University of Liverpool	liverpool.ac.uk

Getting to Liverpool:

Located almost equidistant from London and Edinburgh, Liverpool is within easy reach of all major UK cities as well as Ireland, Scotland and Wales. By air and sea the city also acts as the gateway to Merseyside and England's North West (see maps opposite).

Air

Liverpool John Lennon Airport is just 8 miles from the city centre and has regular scheduled flights to and from more than 60 European destinations with easyjet, Ryanair, VLM, Flybe and Wiz Air.

The Airlink 500 provides a regular bus service to the city centre. (Travel line: 0870 608 2608).

liverpoolairport.com

Manchester Airport offers an international gateway from all parts of the world. There is a direct rail link to Liverpool city centre (journey time 1½ hours). There are regular shuttle flights into Manchester from other major UK airports including Gatwick and Heathrow.

manchesterairport.com

Coach

National Express is located off Norton Street in the city centre (see map on page 172) and operates regular services to and from all major UK towns and cities.

nationalexpress.com

Rail

Regular services run from major towns and cities into Liverpool **Lime Street station** making it one of the most accessible cities within the UK. Journey times from London to Liverpool are just over two hours on Virgin Trains.

For more information contact National Rail on 08457 489950.

thetrainline.co.uk
virgintrains.co.uk

Road

From the M6 Liverpool is easily reached via the M58, M56 and M62 motorways. The city centre is approx. 45 minutes drive from Chester via M53, Manchester and North Wales; just over one hour from Blackpool, the Lake District, Yorkshire Moors, Snowdonia and the Peak District National Parks; just over four hours from London and Edinburgh.

transportdirect.co.uk

Sea

The new **Liverpool Cruise Terminal** opened in September 2007. This port of call facility allows passengers direct access to the city centre of Liverpool and World Heritage site within 5 minutes of disembarkation.

For more information go to:

liverpool08.com/cruise

Services between Liverpool, Douglas, Belfast and Dublin are operated by Norfolk line, P&O Irish Sea and steam packet ferries.

For more details, service times and special offers go to:

norfolkline.com
poirishsea.com
steam-packet.com

To book accommodation in Liverpool contact
+44 (0) 844 870 0123

For further information contact
+44 (0) 151 225 3275 (minicom)
or go to: visitliverpool.com

For more information on Liverpool,
European Capital of Culture '08
go to: liverpool08.com

The River Mersey
melting pot
Adventure
CLIPPER
ALBERT DOCK

architecture

Liverpool and the UK

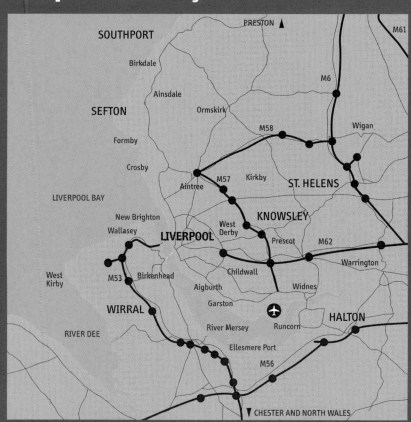

Liverpool and Merseyside

Liverpool City Centre

To best explore Liverpool begin by visiting the Tourist Information Centres at The '08 Place on Whitechapel or The Albert Dock.

For more information contact **+44 (0) 151 233 2008** or go to **liverpool08.com**

Attractions

01	ACC Liverpool
02	Albert Dock
03	Beatles Story
04	Bluecoat
05	Cavern Club
06	Empire Theatre
07	Everyman Theatre
08	FACT
09	International Slavery Museum
10	LIPA
11	Liverpool Cathedral
12	Liverpool Central Library
13	Liverpool Town Hall
13	Maritime Museum
15	Mersey Ferries
16	Metropolitan Cathedral
17	Met Quarter
18	Mr Hardman's Photographic Studio
19	National Conservation Centre
20	Odeon Cinema
21	Open Eye Gallery
22	Passport Office
23	Philharmonic Hall
24	Playhouse Theatre
25	Register Office
26	Royal Court Theatre
27	St.George's Hall
28	Tate Liverpool
29	Tourist Information Centre
30	Underwater Street
31	Unity Theatre
32	UL Victoria Gallery & Museum
33	Walker Art Gallery
34	Western Approaches
35	Williamson Tunnels
36	World Museum Liverpool
37	Cains Brewery

H	Hospital
	Merseyrail
⇌	National Rail
P	Parking
P	Parking - Disabled
NHS	NHS Walk in centre
	Toilets
i	Tourist Information

Hotels

01	Aachen Hotel
02	Blackburne Arms
03	Britannia Adelphi
04	Campanile
05	Crowne Plaza
06	Express by Holiday Inn
07	Feathers
08	Hard Days Night Hotel
09	Hanover Hotel
10	Holiday Inn, (city centre)
11	Hope Street Hotel
12	Ibis/Formule 1
13	International Inn
14	Jurys Inn Hotel
15	Lord Nelson Hotel
16	Malmaison
17	Marriott (city centre)
18	Premier Inn (Albert Dock)
19	Premier Inn (city centre)
20	Print Hotel
21	Racquet Club
22	Radisson SAS
23	Sir Thomas Hotel
24	Staybridge Suites
25	The Liner
26	Thistle
27	YHA Liverpool
28	62 Castle Street

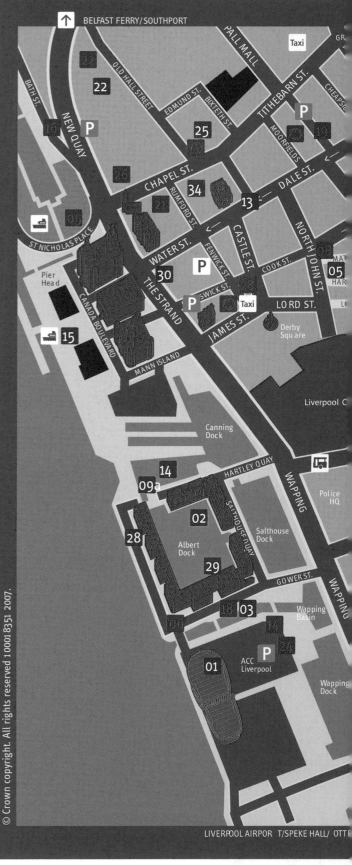

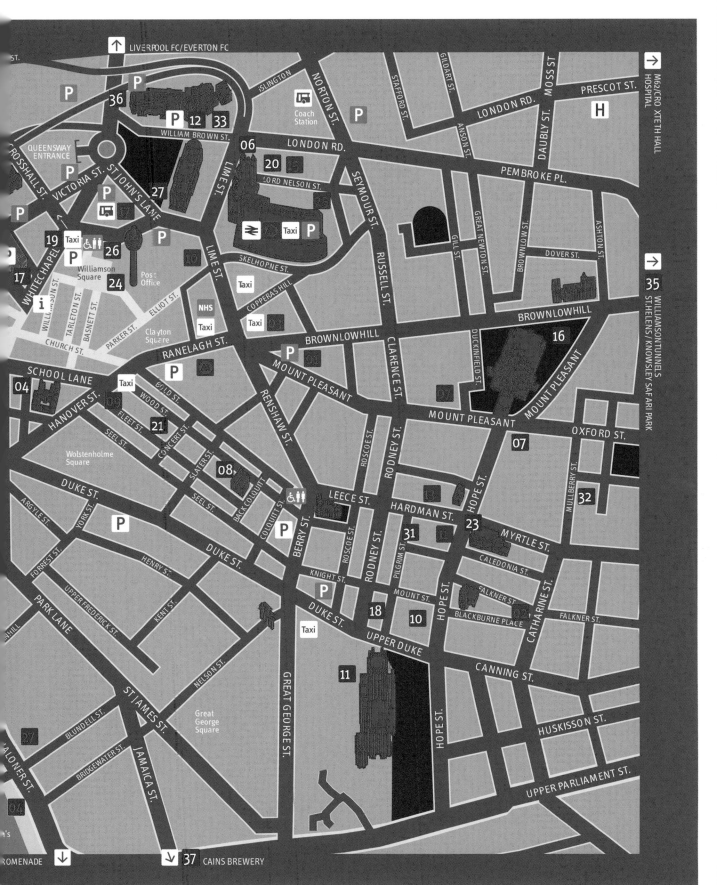

England's Northwest

2008 is an exciting time for England's Northwest.

As Liverpool becomes European Capital of Culture, the rest of the region will be celebrating a series of themed events that highlight the diversity and distinctiveness of the Northwest.

2008 in Manchester will be a Year of World Sport, whilst Cumbria celebrates a Year of Adventure and Cheshire highlights its green heritage through a Year of Gardens. Taste Lancashire '08 is set to put the spotlight on the county's growing food and drink culture.

Manchester's looking up, both figuratively and literally. There's a buzz about the place that means it's as vibrant and immediate as any European capital. The city's now the ideal destination for the cosmopolitan weekender, but its contemporary attitude is still mixed with the down-to earth humour and genuine, no nonsense approach to life that you'd expect in the city that's consistently shown that there are no limits to its imagination and its ambition.

The rolling hills and gentle valleys of the Lancashire countryside have a special charm all of their own, especially when they come dotted with a range of notable restaurants and reinvented country pubs. The area that brought you black pudding, Lancashire cheese, Goosnargh Duck and potted shrimps is rediscovering its culinary heritage, sprouting bistros, farm shops and innovative food producers all over the county.

Chester wears its rich Roman heritage with pride – as you would expect in a city founded by the Romans in AD70. But Chester also has definite contemporary charms, from the slew of new restaurants and boutiques to the tree-lined banks of the River Dee. Outside the city centre, you're straight into the leafy lanes and rolling greenery of the Cheshire countryside, where you'll find no shortage of stately homes and gardens to visit or fine country inns where you can while away a leisurely lunch.

Take it from the mouth of the man himself – of Cumbria, Wordsworth said that there was "nowhere in so narrow a compass with such a variety of the sublime and beautiful." With 16 beautiful lakes, unspoilt beaches and 100 peaks over 2,000 feet high all within a 30-mile stretch, this is the perfect place to go wandering 'lonely as a cloud.'

The joy of the Lakes is that you can leave your boutique hotel, cosy country inn or 5-star restaurant on foot and immediately be in the breathtaking scenery that entranced the poets of yore.

To find out more about how England's Northwest will be celebrating 2008, please read on.

Cheshire's Year of Gardens '08

Cheshire's Year of Gardens '08, an exciting year long festival, will celebrate the rich, dramatic heritage of the Gardens of Distinction and the fresh green environment in Cheshire.

That's because we have more gardens open to the public than anywhere else in the UK, many of international importance, others are simply the result of an urge to create a beautiful and enticing corner of the landscape.

Be dazzled by a world of display! It's not only the bees that are buzzing about our gardens. They are fragrant backdrops for a whole host of cultural events and private parties. From flower shows and music concerts complete with firework displays as impressive and as breathtaking as the blooms.

Pass enchanted evenings by the banks of a lake, or on a rolling lawn, listening to the strains of a beautiful orchestra while imbibing the sweet scents of a summer twilight.

Enjoy live theatre among the flower beds on sunny afternoons or simply 'be there' at the opening of the Secret Garden at Quarry Bank Mill.

Spring and Summer '08 see the start of our Arts Biennial kicking off a season of live music and outdoor theatre. It's also when we launch our National Gardens Scheme where private gardens, including those at the Eaton Estate hold open days.

July is when the world famous RHS Flower Show enjoys its 10th Anniversary with spectacular floral displays at Tatton Park in Chester the Mystery Plays get underway once more.

With the month of September comes the much anticipated National Britain in Bloom Annual Awards. While October brings the North West Fine Foods and Food Lovers' Fair.

The year concludes with Something Wishful in December with romantic lantern parades, music, street arts, dance and fire works.

For more information on Cheshire's Year of Gardens '08 visit yearofgardens08.com

Lake District and Cumbria - Year of Adventure '08

Enjoy a year of living adventurously in the Lake District. With an adrenalin-fuelled calendar of outdoor events, new activities and exciting challenges, '08 is the time to get warmed up and embark on your very own adventure. Dramatic and dynamic. Peaceful and graceful.

The Lake District is a land of extremes. Striking and untamed crags contrast gently undulating slopes. Dense forest opens onto sprawling, bracken cloaked hills. Lofty windswept peaks reflect in still, tranquil lakes. With these extremes of terrain come extremes of pursuit. From a leisurely amble taking in the views, to a full scale trek, taking on.

England's highest mountains. Whether you walk, climb, sail, windsurf, gorge scramble, mountain bike, swim, hang glide, quad bike, horse ride, kayak, or simply sit and watch, you can't help but love this land of diversity.

Embrace your adventurous nature and add a little adrenalin to your life.

For more information on Cumbria and the Lake District's Year of Adventure '08 visit golakes.co.uk/adventure

Taste Lancashire '08 - The Year of Food & Drink

Lancashire celebrates great local produce during '08, in partnership with Liverpool's European Capital of Culture celebrations.

Lancashire and Blackpool Tourist Board is co-ordinating `Taste Lancashire '08`, a wide range of events and promotions including championing up and coming young chefs and raising the quality of eateries in the area.

Taste Lancashire '08 was launched in October '07 in Garstang when the world's biggest Lancashire hotpot was created for the Guinness World Records.

Lloyd Grossman is the Patron of Taste Lancashire '08. Lancashire is renowned for its Morecambe Bay potted shrimps, Lancashire cheese, Lancashire hotpot, Goosnargh chicken, lamb and beef from Bowland and drinks including Sarsaparilla.

Many of the events are in partnership with local produce champions Made in Lancashire and Liverpool's fine eateries.

Liverpool representatives are expected at farmers' markets in Lancashire and at many of the existing and well-supported food festivals including:

- Northcote Manor Festival of Food & Wine (January)
- Taste Lancashire and the Lancashire Food and Drink Festival (April)
- NW Fine Food Lovers Festival at Stonyhurst College (August)
- Pennine Lancashire Festival of Food and Culture (September)
- Garstang and Bowland Banquet (October)

Lancashire's reputation for its range of produce is not surprising considering the county has two areas of outstanding natural beauty - the Forest of Bowland and Arnside and Silverdale, not to mention the West Pennine Moors and 137 miles of coastline including the world famous resort of Blackpool.

More details on the year from tastelancashire08.com

Manchester World Sport '08

2008 is the single biggest year of world sport in Manchester since the XVII Commonwealth Games in 2002.

The city will be hosting a unique series of unmissable championship events. Manchester will be buzzing with passion and adrenalin, as the world's greatest athletes arrive in numbers, ready to test themselves against the best of the best, in pursuit of some of the most prestigious prizes in their sports. Enjoy all the drama and tension of world championship sport at its most exhilarating, in one year, in one city.

If you're in Manchester for one of these unique sporting events, it would be a tragedy to miss the city sights - not forgetting the museums, galleries, theatres, shopping, and unforgettable nightlife.

There's also the finest food and drink in one of the most vibrant café bar, gastro pub and restaurant scenes in the UK.

For more information on Manchester World Sport '08 and to book the perfect sports break, visit manchesterworldsport08.com

For '08 to be successful, we have needed support from a number of public and private sector partners. Together they have played an enormous role in both helping to fund key projects and key elements of the programme and providing resources to make it happen. They are:

LIVERPOOL 08 OFFICIAL PARTNERS

liverpool08.com

OFFICIAL SUPPORTERS

OFFICIAL SUPPLIERS

MAJOR FUNDING PARTNERS

FRIENDS

**Ethel Austin Properties • John Lewis Plc
Beetham Organization Ltd
Mando Group Ltd • Royal Liver Assurance Ltd**

liverpool08.com

The City of Liverpool

United Utilities

United Utilities is proud to support Liverpool's year as European Capital of Culture 2008. This prestigious title has been bestowed on a city, which is in the heart of our operational area. Capital of Culture will benefit the economy, image and reputation in north west England.

Corporate responsibility is an important area for United Utilities helping us take active responsibility for the management of our impact on society and the environment. As a result, it links closely to our approach towards sustainable development. We recognise our responsibilities to the communities where we operate, and to society as a whole. We also support community activity across the company, investing company resources in partnerships and projects where we can share benefits with local communities.

We believe that businesses have a duty to have a positive impact on society and we have been awarded the title Official Community Partner in recognition of our community work in Merseyside. We will continue to develop projects with the community aimed at encouraging the whole of the North West to get behind Liverpool.

Our partnership has enabled us to involve our employees in Liverpool '08 by taking part in community projects with local schools and community groups.

This is a natural continuation of our long-standing support for Liverpool - our wastewater investment has helped transform the Mersey into something the city can be proud of once more - a focal point for the celebrations. We are undertaking one of the largest investment programmes in the UK and will spend £3.2 billion over the next five years.

As part of our sponsorship we are also providing facilities at our Liverpool wastewater treatment works for the '08 volunteers training and this will be a key part of our involvement during '08 along with the use of our leased site at Wellington Dock for the prestigious Tall Ships event in July.

Our partnership enables us to distribute tickets for various events in Merseyside to the community. We are also working closely with the Creative Communities Team at the Culture Company on diverse and cultural projects that will provide sustainable benefits to our communities.

Enterprise
maintaining the infrastructure of the UK

Enterprise is a North West based support services company that provides infrastructure maintenance services for the public sector, the utilities industry and other large organisations throughout the UK

The company in its current form was the result of the merger in 2000 of ARM Services and the AiM quoted Enterprise plc. In 2000 revenue was £100m and is now around £1.2bn a year. Enterprise plc started in 1982 as a public private partnership, one of the first in the UK. It was a joint venture with Lancashire County Council. The aim of the business was to assist with economic regeneration, especially in the North West and performance improvement.

ARM Services was created in 1964 and became a supplier of basic maintenance services to BT. By developing its unique IT and work management systems it was able to develop methods for improving performance and reducing cost for Utility and Public sector customers.

Enterprise has recently acquired Acccrd, another support services company. The combined business will be the largest UK company dedicated to the maintenance of the infrastructure. Through having a larger presence in the UK public sector Enterprise will be able to improve further the innovative, high quality services it provides to Local Authorities and the Highways Agency in the UK.

Our goal remains to achieve best value for the communities in which we operate and to provide services and jobs that are sustainable. The combination of the two businesses will provide many development opportunities for employees.

Services offered by the combined company include:

· Highway Maintenance and Inspection

· Streetscene

· Refuse and Environmental Services including Recycling

· Social Housing Maintenance

· Business Process Re-engineering

We operate a state-of-the-art contact centre in Speke, at The Matchworks. This is bringing jobs and skills development to the city and provides contact centre and work flow management support for contracts throughout the UK. This facility will bring over 800 jobs to the city.

Enterprise is proud to be a sponsor of the Capital of Culture and to work in this unique city. We work in true partnership with Liverpool in EnterpriseLiverpool, a joint venture owned by the city, ourselves and the community. We look forward to the programme of events next year and to working alongside the council and the people of Liverpool in the future.

As an Official Partner of Liverpool, European Capital of Culture '08, the team here at Sayers is bursting with pride and can't wait for the celebrations to begin.

Sayers is the biggest independent retail baker in the north-west, offering our customers a wide range of savouries, sandwiches and specialist bakery products.

The original Sayers business was established in 1912 in Liverpool and in almost 100 years of trading we have grown substantially. We also trade under the Hampsons name in Blackpool, Manchester and Lancashire.

Thousands of satisfied customers are served every day at our shops which stretch from Fleetwood in the north, Macclesfield in the south, to North Wales in the west and Leeds in the east. Our delivery vans cover thousands of miles every day to make sure all of our shops receive the finest quality and freshest pies, pasties, sandwiches and cakes.

We have three types of shops, city centre, suburban and neighbourhood, reflecting changing consumer trends and catering for every customer need and lifestyle.

Sayers makes a valuable contribution to the north-west regional economy. We have more than 200 shops employing around 2,100 trained staff whose high standard of work and professional pride has contributed to the company's success.

Our Liverpool roots mean a lot to us and that is why we were so keen to support the celebrations marking Liverpool as European Capital of Culture. Using the city's 800th birthday as the launch pad for a year of celebrations, we had a great party in August and the next 12 months will be crammed with exciting events and promotions taking place in and around our shops that will celebrate Liverpool's heritage and the part that Sayers has played in it.

We're going to have Liverpool '08 'Ambassadors' in a number of our shops around the city who will be able to provide information about Capital of Culture events and we're even helping to feed the hundreds of volunteers at these events with a range of refreshments and hot and cold drinks.

With almost 100 shops and over 1,000 staff in Liverpool alone, the European Capital of Culture promises to be a big party and the staff here at Sayers can't wait for 2008!

Covering an area rich in both regeneration investment and cultural reinvigoration, the Liverpool Echo has its finger firmly on the pulse of Merseyside. The Liverpool Echo is a regional brand with national recognition, read and enjoyed by hundreds of thousands of people on a daily basis.

The traditional editorial strengths of the Liverpool Echo are now also reflected in two groundbreaking projects - Echo TV, a new monthly magazine programme broadcast in the city's hackney cabs, and featuring celebrity interviews, listings and pieces on regeneration, history and sport, and Street TV, a new headline, picture and video service screened in Church Street in the heart of the city. People on Merseyside have been turning to the Liverpool Daily Post for their news since 1855. It was the first one penny paper launched in the city, and although it merged with its rival publication the Liverpool Mercury in 1904, the Daily Post has always retained the same title.

Throughout its long career it has undergone many changes and redesigns. Today's Daily Post is aimed at professionals and urbanites and those who hold the newspaper in high regard for its integrity and accuracy.

In February 2006, the Liverpool Daily Post and Echo signed a deal to become official partners of European Capital of Culture. Both newspapers had played a crucial role in helping Liverpool to win the culture crown in June 2003 through vigorous campaigning, galvanising the support of the entire region, and welcomed the chance to continue backing the '08 phenomenon.

For '08 the Liverpool Daily Post & Echo will provide unrivalled coverage of the events, spectacles and performances being rolled out throughout the year.

The Liverpool Echo's Arts Editor Joe Riley, Culture Reporter Catherine Jones, and the Liverpool Daily Post's Arts Editor Phil Key will provide extensive previews and reviews, as well as a daily culture diary and extended entertainment sections in both papers. In addition to this, the Echo's new multi-media channels Echo TV and Street TV will also carry comprehensive coverage of the programme.

The titles websites will enable users to feel a part of 2008, wherever they live.

liverpooldailypost.co.uk and liverpoolecho.co.uk will give readers a comprehensive guide to 2008, featuring exclusive photo galleries along with video and audio packages of key events. The Liverpool Echo and Liverpool Daily Post are part of the fabric of Liverpool and will play a hugely important role in providing the oxygen of publicity to the 08 programme of activity - and beyond. The titles are read by three quarters of the population on Merseyside and will play a key role in galvanising the local community - readers and advertisers - at this crucial time for the city.

The Liverpool Echo and Daily Post are proud to be adding support to this wonderful adventure. As an official partner, it will enable the titles to play an integral part in what is going to be an exciting year by providing extensive exposure to the '08 programme.

Merseytravel

Merseytravel is the official transport partner of Liverpool' European Capital of Culture 2008, an event that will showcase the city on a global stage.

We want people to know what we know, that Liverpool is one of the world's great cities and can host a fantastic year long party.

What we also know is that transport will play a vital part in the celebrations.

Part of our commitment to Liverpool '08, will be to ensure that public transport continues to work successfully to move visitors and local people around many of the key events taking place during the year.

As well as serving the transport needs of the city, we are making an artistic investment that includes public art works, topiaries and buskers at key gateways to the city.

Liverpool's transport system has been involved in significant improvements in the approach to the '08 celebrations including a £2m facelift for Liverpool Lime Street Station and the development of a stunning new £10m Pier Head Ferry Terminal.

The diversity of Liverpool's transport network may surprise visitors who have never been to the city before and we plan to use everything from our world famous Mersey Ferries, our UK-leading rail network, bus stations, travel centres and two Mersey Tunnels to the fullest, to support '08.

There will be banners at Lime Street and a programme of our own events to support the wider 2008 line-up, including special ferry cruises, tunnel tours and a rare walk-through of the Queensway Tunnel.

Last year, around 200 million passenger journeys were made on public transport and in '08 that number to be even greater with the extra influx of visitors, whose first impressions of the city may well be shaped by their arrival by public transport.

Merseytravel is the joint Merseyside Passenger Transport Authority (MPTA) and Executive (MPTE). Covering the area of Merseyside - the five districts of Liverpool, Wirral, St Helens, Knowsley and Sefton - Merseytravel co-ordinates public transport, working in partnership with bus and rail operators to provide local solutions for local challenges.

Every day, Merseytravel is making it easier for people who live, work and visit Merseyside to get to where they want to go easily and cost-effectively.

Our mission is to promote an integrated transport network, accessible to everyone, to improve the quality of life on Merseyside.

BT's sponsorship of the Capital of Culture 2008 builds upon the strategic partnership it has with Liverpool City Council and BT's social and economic investment in the region. Merseyside is a key region for BT. It supports over 25,000 jobs in the North West and last year generated £875 million for the area.

Together, Liverpool City Council and BT have achieved some tremendous successes over the past few years. In 2001, the two organisations entered into a groundbreaking new partnership and a Joint Venture company, known as Liverpool Direct Ltd was formed. The partnership - the largest of its kind in the UK - was set up to help the Council achieve its "seaport to e-port" vision and to improve and modernise the way the Local Authority provided services to its citizens. BT invested over £58m in new technology and business process re-engineering which helped to transform the customer experience for the citizens of Liverpool, by eliminating backlogs and reducing customer waiting times dramatically. Further investments, plus a recent extension to the Partnership will save the region's taxpayers around £48m. Liverpool Direct Ltd has developed rapidly as a company and now works in partnership with many other organisations in the public, private and community sectors.

More recently, November 2007 saw Liverpool become one of the first 'wireless cities' in the UK, bringing fast internet and email access to those on the move.

Through BT's unrivalled Openzone service, local residents, tourists and businesses can work, talk, play, listen and see at broadband speeds in key WiFi enabled locations across the city.

Looking to the future, the new world of 21st Century Network (21CN) comes to parts of the region soon, with full roll out scheduled for completion by 2011. 21CN means that customers will be able to access any communications service from any device, anywhere - and at triple the fastest broadband speeds currently available for most UK customers. People will have greater choice and control over the services they use as a whole range of new services are developed to suit the way we live and work today and in the future.

For example, BT Vision combines the appeal of TV with the interactivity of broadband - customers will be able to watch what they want when they want and not be tied to TV schedules. Convergence is the future for communications and 21CN is designed to make it simple and easy.

2008 will be a fantastic opportunity for Liverpool to showcase itself to the world. By hosting the European Capital of Culture, Liverpool will play a major part in bringing economic growth and regeneration to the region. BT is proud to be an official partner and is delighted to support this important event.

Love every second

Virgin Trains which operates high speed, high quality train services between Liverpool and London is proud to be an Official Partner of Liverpool, European Capital of Culture '08.

Virgin Trains Commercial Director Graham Leech said: "We are delighted to be supporting Liverpool and its community as an Official Partner of the prestigious Capital of Culture. There are going to be some amazing events in 2008 and we look forward to getting involved. And, the Capital of Culture year is just the start, we are committed to improving the region for the long-term with more trains and slashed journey times from 2009".

Virgin currently operates 15 trains each way on weekdays on the Liverpool-London route. However, from 2009 we will be adding three more trains each way and around 25 minutes will be slashed from the journey time. Most trains will take just two hours and seven minutes to complete the 192 mile journey with the fastest train of the day taking just two hours. Over 340,000 extra sets will be provided on the Liverpool-London route every year and there will also be a more regular direct train service at weekends.

In 2007 passenger numbers increased by 14% percent, with almost 20,000 journeys being made every week between London and Liverpool. In the same year the average fare paid dropped by over 13% as more passengers are taking advantage of the cheaper advance fares on offer. Across its entire network Virgin Trains offers over 170,000 advance tickets every week.

What's more, Virgin Pendolino trains emit on average 76% less CO_2 than cars and domestic flights*. So it is hardly surprising that rail has become the travel mode of choice for journeys to and from London, with thousands of passengers voting with their feet and turning their back on domestic air routes.

Through our support of the year long celebrations we will be making it even easier to reach the city and join in the fun with fares from as little as £12.50** one way from London, So there's no excuse not to get up to the Capital of Culture in '08.

*'Greener' statement based on CO2 emissions study (Study by ECCM Ltd. based on flights between London, Manchester, Glasgow and Liverpool and an average car journey). Source: Independent analysis by the Edinburgh Centre for Carbon Management.

** Based on a standard value advance fare from London to Liverpool valid at the time of going to print.

Claire McColgan
Executive Producer-Participation,
Liverpool Culture Company

Fiona Gasper
Executive Producer-Artistic,
Liverpool Culture Company

"We would like to thank all those who have been working on creating and contributing to Liverpool's European Capital of Culture programme in so many ways over the past five years. It has been a privilege to have worked with so many talented people to capture the essence of this city, its cultural landscape, its collective artistic ambition and its communities which reinforce Liverpool's place as a centre of creativity. The programme you see has its roots in Liverpool, but looks to Europe and the world."

Liverpool Culture Company would like to thank all the following:

i Sport Marketing, I.M.Marsh Campus, ICDC, International Paralympic, Nigel Jamieson, Helen Johnson, Kim Johnson, Richard Johnson, Ben Johnstone, Karen Jones, Janice Judd, Ian Jukes, Jump Ship Rat, Jenny Kane, Kinetic Fallacy, Kinetophone Records, Barbara King, Kings Garden, Sarah Klaveness, Knowsley Metropolitan Borough Council, Knowsley Flower Show, Lancashire County Cricket Club, Lateral Visions, Frederike Lavin, Bernice Law, Lawn Tennis Association, LCAD, Le Nouvel Ensemble Moderne, Susan Lees, Alison Leese, Sylvia Lestquoit, Lorraine Lett, Michael Leyland, Lincoln Center Festival, Livepool Tennis Centre, Liverpool & Merseyside Schools, Liverpool Arabic Arts Festival, Liverpool Arts and Culture Network, Liverpool Arts Regeneration Consortium, Liverpool Association of Secondary Heads, Liverpool Biennial, Liverpool Cathedral, Liverpool Central Library, Liverpool Chess Foundation, Liverpool Chinese Community, Liverpool City Council, Liverpool Comedy Festival 2008, Liverpool Comedy Trust, Liverpool Community Games, Liverpool Council of Voluntary Services, Liverpool Cricket Club, Liverpool Empire Theatre, Liverpool Everyman and Playhouse Theatres, Liverpool Football Club, Liverpool Fringe Festival, Liverpool Gymnastics Centre of Excellence, Liverpool Handball Club, Liverpool Hope University, Liverpool Institute for Performing Arts, Liverpool Irish Festival, Liverpool John Moore University, Liverpool Lantern Festival, Liverpool Lesbian & Gay Film Festival, Liverpool Central Library, Liverpool Lighthouse, Liverpool Medical Institute, Liverpool Music Week, Liverpool Olympia, Liverpool PCT, Liverpool Philharmonic Hall, Liverpool Primary Care NHS Trust, Liverpool Primary Heads Association, Liverpool Reads, Liverpool Samba School, Liverpool Slavery Remembrance Initiative, Liverpool Theatres Trust, Liverpool University Press, Liverpool Weekend Arts College, Liverpool Welsh Choral, Liverpool Young Promoters, Liverpool Youth Service, Lodestar Theatre Company, Claire Lofthouse, London Artists Project, Kathryn Luke, Jackie Malcolm, Anna Maloney, Kim Maloney, Manchester International Arts, Rob March, Sarah Maudsley, Sue McAdam, Victoria McCauley, Claire McColgan, Suzanne McDonough, Mark McKenna, Andy McNicholl, Cathy Meadows, Mello Mello Jazz Café, Brenda Mellor, Mersey Care NHS Trust, Merseyside Dance Initiative, Mersey Film and Video, Merseyside Fire & Rescue Service, Merseyside Music Development Agency, Merseyside Police, Merseyside Sport Partnership, Metal Liverpool, Metropolitan Cathedral of Christ the King, Milapfest, Kimberley Mitchell, Lorraine Molyneux, Momentum, John Moore, More Music, Richard Morgan, Roy Morris, MTV, Frank Murphy, Jackie Murray, Musical Youth, MZONE, National Garden Society, National Holocaust Museum, National Museums Liverpool, National Trust, National Wildflower Centre, Nationale Loterji, Neighbourhood Management Teams of Liverpool City Council, Neutral Spoon, New Brighton Promenade, New Brighton RUFC, Paul Newman, Noise Festival, Chris Noon, Norris Green Youth Centre Ltd, Northern Vision, Northwest Vision + Media, Novas Comtemporary Urban Centre, Novas Group, Nutkhut, NWDAF and DaDa Fest, Nicola O'Boyle, Angela O'Hare, James O'Keeffe, Onteca, Open Eye Gallery, Opera Frankfurt, Opéra National de Paris, Ossie Omar, Osun Arts Foundation, Tracy Owen, Pacific Road Arts Centre, Pagoda Chinese Youth Orchestra, Parks and Environment Service of Liverpool City Council, Anne Parris, People Show, Neil Peterson, Roger Philips, Planet Darts, Lauren Poland, Positive Impact, Ben Potter, Rachel Powell, Steve Power, Primary Care Trust, Kim Rawlinson, Red Dot Exhibitions ltd/Colin Serjent, Angie Redhead, Phil Redmond, Janet Reeder, RIBA Trust, Richard Alston Dance Company, Catherine Rigby, River Media, Gordon Ross, Rotunda College, Royal and Ancient Golf Club, Royal Birkdale, Royal Court, Royal Liverpool Philharmonic Orchestra,

Royal National Theatre, Russell Maliphant Company, Nancy Rutherford, Irene Ryan, Sail Training Internaitional, Lynne Saunders, Neil Scales, Sir Bob Scott, Scottish Dance Theatre, Peter Seddon, Sefton Metropolitan Borough Council, Sefton Park Palm House, Sense of Sound, Sharon Sephton, Val Shaw, Sherdlry Park, Julie Sherry, Shobaba Jeyasingh Dance Company, Singh Twins, Skylight Projects - The Royal Standard, Kathryn Smith, Alicia Smith, Society of Antiquaries of London, Sound Network, Southport Arts Centre, Southport Flower Show, Alan Southward, Speedminton UK, Spike Theatre, Sport England, St George's Hall, St Helens Eclectica, St Helens RLFC, St Helens Council, Stadt Moers Park, Mark Stewart, Mike Storey, Alastair Stott, Sudley House, Sydvest Film, T&M, Table Tennis Committee, TAG (The Artists Group), Myriam Tahir, Tara Parks Travellers Community, Tate Liverpool, Phil Taylor, Team a go-go, Tenant Spin, The Art Organisation (TAO), The Athene Trust, The Bluecoat, The Brindley, The British Association of Science, The Citadel, The Cornerstone Gallery, The Cultures of Childhood Network, The European Opera Centre, The Festival d'Automne à Paris, The Greenhouse Multi-Cultural Play and Arts Project, The Hive Collective, The Jockey Club, The Muslim Cultural Festival of Liverpool, The National Ballet of China, The National Wildflower Centre, The New Picket, The New Works Theatre Company, The Poetry Society, The Reader, The Royal Standard, The Singh Twins, The Tour of Britain, The Windows Project, The Youth Arts Friendship Field, Theater Festival Boulevard, Dave Thomas, Jackie Thompson, Time Circus, Time Circus and Laika, Tom of Finland Foundation, Peter Toyne, Toxteth TV, Tranmere Rovers Football Club, John Turner, Julie Turner, Elaine Turpin, Julia Turpin, Sebastian Tyrakowski, UK Film Council, unitytheatre, University of Liverpool, UPM, Urban Cultural Network, Urban Strawberry Lunch, Robbie Valentine, Sarah Vasey, Helen Vickers, Victoria Gallery & Museum, Victoria Park, Visit Chester and Cheshire, Walk the Plank, Alan Walsh, Waterloo RUFC, Wavertree Athletics Centre, Wellington Street School Building, Tony Wells, Welsh National Opera, Susan Whitehead, Wicked Fish Theatre Company, Widnes RLFC, Wienerfestwochen, Wild in Art, Clare Wilde, Mat Wilkinson, Ashley Williams, Anita Williams, Eileen Willshaw, Tony Wilson, Wirral Metropolitan Borough Council, Sue Woodward, World Squash Federation, Gaynor Wright, Writing On the Wall, Yellow House, Youth Music, Zho Visual Theatre.

And a final and heartfelt thank you to all the artists, poets, writers, performers, actors and actresses, musicians, singers, sportsmen and women, comics, academics, scientists, designers, directors, producers, technical support - and last but not least the people of Liverpool and Merseyside, who all together will make 08 a year like no other.

Image credits:

AL and AL, Another Media, Arts Council London, Patrick Baldwin, Jon Barraclough, Bedford Lemere & Co, Wonge Bergmann, Jyll Bradley, Adrian Burrows, Estate of Stanley Spencer/DACS 2007, Louise Clark, Phil Collins, Ben Crompton, Anthony Crooks, Yannick Demmerle, Dave Evans, Chris Floyd, Carlos Furman, FACT, Dennis Gilbert, Hugo Glendinning, Simmy Gupta, Tony Hardacre, E. Chambre Hardman, Ben Harries, Mat Henneck - EMI Classics, Larry Hickmott, Liu Chen-Hsiang, Ian Jackson of Art in Liverpool, Julian James, Graham Jepson, Gregory King, K@osmos by Grupo Puja, Gavin Lamb, Liverpool Biennial, Little Brown Book Group, Liverpool Empire, Liverpool Everyman and Playhouse Theatres, Manet, Mary McCartney, Mark McNulty, Terry Mealey, Memento Mori, MTV, National Museums Liverpool, National Trust, Zadoc Nava, Nutkhut, October Communications, Dai Owen, Eryl Parry, Michael Peto, Photocritic, Raphael Pierre, Press Association, Villa Savoye, Philharmonic Hall, Poissey, Bernard Préfontaine , Simon Richardson, Bridget Riley, Sefton Park Palm House Trust, Brian Slater, Christian Smith, Keith Smith, Tim Smith, John Stezaker, Tate, Javier Téllez, Galerie Peter Kilchmann of Zurich, Villa Savoye, Tissue Culture and Art (FACT: sk-Interfaces), Tom of Finland, Trinity Mirror, Tyngdkraft, var min vän, Schwerkraft, sei meine Freundin, Pipilotti Rist, Johan Warden, Hauser & Wirth Zürich London, unitytheatre, Jasmin Vardimon, Virgin Books, Matej Andraz Vogrincic, Wild in Art, Alex Wolkowicz, McCoy Wynne.

Other credits:

Designed by: Finch, printed by: Trinity Mirror, paper supplied by: UPM-Kymmene (UK) Ltd.

This publication provides a flavour of the highlights of
Liverpool's year as European Capital of Culture 2008.
It is not the definitive programme.

In conjuntion with this publication, a series of seasonal
guides will be published to provide the latest up-to-date news
and information on all events. These seasonal guides can be
found in Liverpool's Tourist Information Centres and selected
cultural venues.

For more information contact +44 (0) 151 233 2008 or go to
liverpool08.com.

Liverpool Culture Company,
PO Box 2008, Municipal Buildings,
Dale Street, Liverpool L2 2DH

Tel: +44 (0) 151 233 4399
Fax: +44 (0) 151 233 6333
Email: contact@liverpool08.com
web: liverpool08.com

This publication is available in large print,
Braille or translation.

To obtain your copy please contact Liverpool
direct on +44 (0) 151 233 2008.

PTO - For the cultural stepping stones to a year of surprises...

Published in Great Britain in 2008 by: Trinity Mirror

ISBN 978-1-9052-66401

Printed and finished by Scotprint, Haddington, Scotland

Designed and produced by Finch 0151 236 2134

'08 Calendar

All Year

To February '09
Liverpool's Public Art
Programme inc. Winter
Lights Series and Pavilions

To Spring '09
The Twentieth Century:
How it Looked and How
it Felt
Tate Liverpool, Albert Dock

To 27 September '09
Merseyside Maritime
Museum, Albert Dock

Leeds-Liverpool Canal,
Sefton and North Liverpool

Various venues

**Last Thursday
of every month**
Albert Dock

Various events

Liverpool and Nationwide

St George's Heritage Centre,
St John's Lane

FACT, Wood Street
and city wide

Various venues

Liverpool Schools

Fitzcarraldo, Canning Dock

Disability Sports Festival
Various venues

Visible Virals:
Urban Virals, Parks Virals
Various venues

Waiting
Various venues

January

To 13
The Turner Prize 07
Tate Liverpool, Albert Dock

To 19
John Stezaker
Open Eye, Wood Street

To 26
Empire Theatre, Lime Street

To 31
Picton Library Reading Room,
William Brown Street

To 2 March
National Conservation Centre,
Whitechapel, Liverpool

To 16 March
Lady Lever Art Gallery,
Port Sunlight, Wirral

To July
The Infinite Sea
of Possibilities

To Autumn
Merchant Palaces
Sudley House, Mossley Hill

1 - 5
St George's Concert Room,
William Brown Street

3 - 5
Philharmonic Hall,
Hope Street

4
Philharmonic Hall,
Hope Street

5
The Wayne Shorter
Quartet with the RLPO
Philharmonic Hall,
Hope Street

5 - 7 February
The Anne Frank Festival
Liverpool Cathedral,
St James Mount

5 - 17
Treasures Exhibition
St George's Heritage Centre,
St John's Lane

11
St George's Plateau,
Lime Street

12
ECHO Arena Liverpool,
Kings Dock

14
St George's Hall,
Lime Street

24
St George's Hall, Lime Street

25 - 26
ECHO Arena Liverpool,
Kings Dock

25 - 16 February
Everyman Theatre,
Hope Street

25 - 22 March
Open Eye, Wood Street

27
Philharmonic Hall,
Hope Street

31 - 2 February
Empire Theatre, Lime Street
and various venues

February

1 - 30 March
sk-interfaces
FACT, Wood Street

5 - 9
Anima by Momentum
unitytheatre,
Hope Place

10
Chinese New
Year Celebrations
Chinatown, Nelson Street

18
Roscoe Lecture -
City of Sculpture
St George's Hall,
Lime Street

26
TWINS Auditions
the Bluecoat, School Lane

28
Liverpool Metropolitan
Cathedral, Mount Pleasant

29 - 10 April
Novas Contemporary Urban
Centre, Greenland Street

March

1
Liverpool Welsh Choral
Union with Aled Jones
Philharmonic Hall
Hope Street

1 - 15
LEAP Festival
Various venues

6 onwards
City wide

7 - 8
Akram Khan - bahok
Liverpool Playhouse,
Williamson Square

8
English Schools
Cross-country
Championships
Sefton Park,
Croxteth Drive

11
Circelation

13 - 16
International Table
Tennis Tournament
Greenbank Sports Academy,
Greenbank Lane

14
Globalization -
The Making of Our World
St George's Concert Room,
William Brown Street

14 - 15
The Long Walk
The Cornerstone,
Haigh Street

15
Karl Jenkins Stabat Mater
Liverpool Cathedral,
St James Mount

15 - 4 May
Now Then
the Bluecoat,
School Lane

19
Roscoe Lecture -
City of Music
St George's Hall,
Lime Street

19
'08 Carnival
Olympiad Seminar
The Cornerstone,
Haigh Street

20
'08 Premier Darts
ECHO Arena Liverpool,
Kings Dock

30
European Union
Youth Orchestra
Philharmonic Hall,
Hope Street

All Day and All
Night - Premiere
Liverpool

April

To September
Around the City
in Eighty pubs

To September
Out of the Shadows
St George's Heritage Centre,
St Johns Lane

To December
Twilight City
Various venues

1 - 2
Ken Dodd and Liverpool's
Laughter Makers
St George's Concert Room,
William Brown Street

3 - 5
The Grand National
Aintree Racecourse
Ormskirk Road

7 - 10 May
One Step Forward,
One Step Back
Liverpool Cathedral,
St James Mount

7 - 12
Wirral Bookfest
Venues around Wirral

7 - 30 November
Liverpool's People and
Places the Photography
of E. Chambré Hardman
Various venues

11 - 3 May
Endgame
Everyman Theatre,
Hope Street

12 - 13
Viennese Balls
St George's Hall,
Lime Street

17 - 18
Into the Little Hill:
A Lyric Tale in Two Parts
Pacific Roads Arts Centre,
Birkenhead

18 - 8 June
AL and AL
FACT, Wood Street

18 - 10 August
Art in the Age of Steam
Walker Art Gallery,
William Brown Street

22 - 27
People Show 119:
Ghost Sonata
The Palm House,
Sefton Park, Croxteth Drive

24
The Shankly Show
Liverpool Olympia,
West Derby Road

26
Rotunda Pavilion
Vauxhall

28
The Business Convention
Arena and Convention Centre
Liverpool, Kings Dock

29
Roscoe Lecture -
Reflections and Changes
St George's Hall,
Lime Street

Late April - early May
Poetry in the City
Various venues

May

To August
Four Corners
Various venues

To October
Parks Virals

Throughout May
Writing on the
Wall Festival
Various venues

1
Ecce Cor Meum
Liverpool Cathedral,
St James Mount

1 - 3
Intercultural Cities
Conference
BT Conference Centre,
Kings Dock

2
Metal Pavilion
Edge Hill Station, Kensington

3 - 5
Happy 20th Birthday
Tate Liverpool
Albert Dock

6 - 12
British Open Squash
Championships
Liverpool Cricket Club,
Aigburth Drive and ECHO
Arena Liverpool, Kings Dock

9 - 31
Tartuffe (adapted
by Roger McGough)
Liverpool Playhouse,
Williamson Square

15
Roscoe Lecture -
City of Fashion
St George's Hall,
Lime Street

17
An Evening
with Bryn Terfel
Philharmonic Hall,
Hope Street

17 - 18
HUB Festival
Otterspool Park,
Otterspool Drive

24
Voices Across the Ocean,
Liverpool Welsh Choral
Mossley Hill Parish Church,
Rose Lane

24 - 2 November
Liverpool Cityscape
by Ben Johnson
Walker Art Gallery
William Brown Street

24 - 25
European Speedminton
Championships '08
Liverpool Tennis Centre,
Wellington Road

24 - 25
Liverpool International
Handball Festival
Greenbank Sports Academy,
Greenbank Lane and I. M.
Marsh Campus

24 - 26
Liverpool Streets Ahead
St George's Plateau
and city centre

24 - 30
International
Pop Overthrow
Various venues

28 - 8 June
Liverpool
Comedy Festival
Various venues

29 - 1 June
Southport International
Jazz Festival
Various venues

30 - 31 August
Gustav Klimt: Painting,
Design and Modern Life
in Vienna 1900
Tate Liverpool, Albert Dock

31
Garston Pavilion
Wellington Street School

31
National Junior Open
Karate Tournament
Greenbank Sports Academy,
Greenbank Lane

Physical Fest 4
Various venues

June

To August
Streetwaves
City wide

1
The Liverpool Sound
Anfield Stadium

4 - 11
The Big Hope
Hope University,
Hope Park Campus
and various venues

7
Lord Mayor's Parade
Liverpool city centre

7 - 8
Kites Over the Mersey
New Brighton promenade,
Wirral

8
The Green Fayre
Court Hey Park,
Roby Road, Huyton

9
Roscoe Lecture -
Where Religious Faith
is Part of the Solution,
Not the Problem
St George's Hall,
Lime Street

10 - 15
Liverpool
International Tennis
Calderstones Park,
Menlove Avenue

12 - 14
Magical Mysterious
Regeneration Tour
The University
of Liverpool

Alice in Wonderland
Liverpool 14-15
Knowsley 21-22
Halton 28-29

4 - 14
Festival of Hope '08
Hope Street

14
Der Rosenkavalier,
Philharmonic Hall
Hope Street

16 - 25 August
Go Superlambananas
City wide

19
Roscoe Lecture -
City of Media
St George's Hall,
Lime Street

19-22
Design Show Liverpool
The Crypt, Metropolitan
Cathedral, Brownlow Hill

21 - 22
Africa Oyé
Sefton Park

25 - 26
Knowsley Hall
Music Festival

27 - 31 August
Pipilotti Rist
FACT, Wood Street

28
War Requiem by
Benjamin Britten
Liverpool Cathedral,
St James Mount

28 - 9 November
Masterpiece
Watercolours
and Drawings
Lady Lever Art Gallery,
Port Sunlight

28 - 19 July
Once Upon a Time
at the Adelphi
Liverpool Playhouse,
Williamson Square

29
Liverpool Open Gardens
The Palm House, Sefton
Park and other venues

Liverpool Open
Source City
Various venues

July

To August
Movieplex - World Cinema
in a Nutshell

To August
Hopes Street Ltd
Public Art Programme
Speke and Garston

1 - 31
Liverpool Summer Pops
ECHO Arena Liverpool

4
Clipper Round-the-
World-Yacht-Race
Mersey Waterfront

5
Chinese Dub
Carling Academy,
Hotham Street

5
Merseyside
Youth Games
Wavertree Sports Complex,
Wellington Road

5 - 6
St Helens Festival
Sherdley Park, Marshalls
Cross Road, Sutton

10 - 27
Liverpool Arabic
Arts Festival
Various venues

10 - 7 September
Arab Cities
the Bluecoat, School Lane
and Open Eye Gallery,
Wood Street

12 - 13
The Wirral Show
New Brighton

12 - 13
Halton Youth
Culture Festival
Halton Stadium, Widnes

12 - 1 November '09
The Beat Goes On
World Museum Liverpool,
William Brown Street

15 - 26
Everyword
Everyman Theatre,
Hope Street

17 - 20
Open Golf Championship
Royal Birkdale,
Waterloo Road, Southport

17 - 24
European Youth
Parliament
St George's Hall, Lime Street

18
John Lennon Song
Book and RLPO
Philharmonic Hall,
Hope Street

18 - 21
Tall Ships' Races '08
Waterfront

18 - 21
International
Shanty Festival
Liverpool Albert and
Wellington Docks

20 - 2 August
Brouhaha International
Street Festival
Various venues

22 - 25
4-Nations Junior
Chess Championships
I.M.Marsh Campus

25 - 27
YPPT International
Conference
The Cornerstone,
Haigh Street

27 - 2 August
Contacting the World
Various venues

27 - 9 August
British Chess
Championships
St George's Hall,
Lime Street